The Beauty of Eating Well ™

BY CAMILLE KNOWLES ™

"Congratulations Camille on creating this wonderful cookbook of beautiful recipes for those wishing to see the benefits of glowing skin. We at CNM believe health is accessed from within, that food is medicine and medicine is food, and that there is no greater joy in life than overcoming an obstacle. Well done for using your qualifications and skills unselfishly: to educate, to help, and to reach others. I wish you the best in this journey, for this is only the beginning."

Hermann Keppler
Principal, College of Naturopathic Medicine
London, UK

Printed in the United Kingdom

First Printing, 2019

ISBN: 978-1-9161783-2-8 (Paperback)
ISBN: 978-1-9161783-3-5 (Hardback)
ISBN: 978-1-9161783-4-2 (eBook)

CMGK IPR Ltd
Lancashire, PR6 9AF

www.thebeautyofeczema.com

How The Beauty of Eczema™ Has Changed Lives

"We are so thankful to have found The Beauty of Eczema™ as it now feels like we have been given the tools to move forward alongside eczema rather than fighting against it. Amelie says: Camille's book is an inspiration and she is too. She has helped me to understand that eczema is not my enemy and is actually my friend. Since finding Camille I feel like I have someone to relate to." — **Marie Smith, mother of Amelie age 10**

"I have never read something that has related to me so much, I sat and cried tears of joy that I am not alone and how honest you are is inspirational. The HOPE Principles in the book have made me make small changes to my lifestyle that have paid off massively!" — **Emily Nicholas**

"The Beauty of Eczema™ Book, Positive Vibes Self-Care Affirmation Cards and The Positive Scribes Journal have been so uplifting and useful in changing my mindset when dealing with my eczema! I no longer feel alone and I know that it won't beat me! They have given me tools on how I can manage my eczema on a daily basis but also that if I have a flare up it's not a big deal. I just need to take a step back and look at what may have caused this. The cards along with the Positive Scribes Journal have played a big part in keeping a positive mindset. The Self-Affirmation Cards are the perfect size to have in my handbag so that if I'm having a difficult day I can just grab them and refocus on all of the positives rather than the negatives! I could not recommend The Beauty of Eczema™ products enough, they have made a huge difference to how I deal with my eczema." — **Eleanor Burnside**

"I don't suffer with eczema but the HOPE Principles apply to everyone. They don't just help you with skin, they help you with stress management, confidence and well-being in general." — **Katie Harrison**

"Finding The Beauty of Eczema™ was the best thing in the world. I needed a mindset shift and the HOPE Principles were the pieces I needed. I am so much better now and so grateful for the positive messages Camille shares with all us warriors." — **Johannao Ojamäe**

"I would place The Beauty of Eczema™ by Camille Knowles on the same level as The Power of Now by Eckhart Tolle – taking charge of the now to the best of your ability and living your best positive life, anyone with any type of skin disorder should read Camille's book." — **Aramide, MyAtopicSkin**

Contents

Introduction

Focus on The JOY of food, eat well and GLOW!

Hey beautiful warrior, my name is Camille Knowles. I am the author and founder of The Beauty of Eczema™, a guide to living a life beyond eczema using the HOPE Principles.

The HOPE Principles provide a framework for how to live your best life beyond eczema, taking into account your mind, body and soul. The Beauty of Eating Well™ is only one part of living a life beyond eczema, but it's a vital ingredient.

My Story

I have lived with eczema since I was six years old and I confess it now; I tried to control my skin via a series of strict diets. There wasn't a food fad, regime or elimination plan I didn't try; alkaline only, nightshade-free, gluten-free, paleo, fruitarian, juicing, ayurvedic etc. At the end of it all I had gained an encyclopaedic knowledge of food and drink, and had varying success with controlling my eczema. But you know what? I was deeply suffering from a fear of food.

Food – the wonderful substance that I had enjoyed throughout my childhood, with fruit trees in our French garden and family dinners al fresco – had become a set of rules to follow.

Eating out was a social minefield, family dinners I tried to control, trips to a new environment left me in a panic.

I reached a point where I was living in fear of anything I put in my mouth. Then, I finally realised: *To live a happy and full life, I need to live a life beyond eczema and part of that was eating food from a place of JOY.*

Since we know mood and environment can influence our skin as much as products and exercise, how about embracing the concept of *eating food that brings you JOY?*

It was a huge turning point for me. Since writing The Beauty of Eczema™, many eczema warriors have been in touch to ask: *What do you eat on a day-to-day basis? How did you relearn to love food AND keep your eczema at bay? Which foods give you such glowing skin?*

This book of recipes combines everything I have learned over the years and I hope it will provide a defining moment for you, beautiful warrior, as it did for me.

Ask yourself, what food brings you JOY? It might be a new concept to you, I know. But try it. And no, I don't mean in the moment, I mean long term. We can feel delight at eating lots of sweets and junk food, but an hour later? Not so much, right? The foods in this book bring me real joy because they are colourful, flavoursome, nutritious, wholesome, fuel me with energy and make my skin GLOW.

Let's try something new together my angels.

Lots of love and positive foodie vibes,

Camille x x

The Essential Selection – Core Foods That I Do and Don't Thrive On

Given that eczema is an inflammatory autoimmune disease you soon learn what is a trigger for your skin. I choose to embrace the amazing foods below that taste great, energise me and lead to glowing skin. Plus I have listed a few that also seem to be a trigger for me that I choose not to eat.

The Food I Embrace:

- >> Fresh berries, avocados, lemons, bananas, figs, mangos and blueberries ... I love fruit!
- >> Fresh colourful vegetables
- >> Gluten-free grains, quinoa, buckwheat, gluten-free oats and wholegrain rice
- >> Fermented foods such as sauerkraut and kimchi
- >> All beans are OK, but I like to soak them first and love to use them for hummus dips
- >> Nuts and seeds, activated whenever possible. Pumpkin seeds are full of zinc. Flax and chia seeds are full of omega-3 fatty acids
- >> Any dairy-free milks including almond, hemp, coconut, cashew, rice and tiger milk
- >> Organic, grass-fed animal protein such as chicken and occasionally beef and lamb
- >> All organic fish – my favourites are salmon, shellfish and anchovies
- >> Coconut yogurt
- >> Sweeteners – raw honey/maple syrup (in moderation)
- >> Oils – olive oil, coconut oil, avocado oil and sesame seed oil
- >> Apple cider vinegar and rice wine vinegar
- >> All herbs
- >> Raw chocolate – yum!

Drinks I Embrace

>> Spring water
>> Hot water and lemon
>> Herbal teas
>> Leaf teas
>> Dairy-free lattes
>> Dairy-free colourful mylks
>> Fresh, cold-pressed fruit or vegetable juices or smoothies
>> Kombucha – a probiotic fizzy drink

Foods I Intuitively Don't Choose (refined sugar, dairy, gluten)

>> Gluten containing grains such as wheat, couscous, oats, bran, barley, rye and spelt
>> Dairy products
>> Factory farmed meats, such as hot dogs, pork and cold cuts
>> Processed and fried food
>> Artificial sweeteners or refined sugars
>> Sunflower oil, canola oil or margarine
>> Commercial salad dressings or sauces
>> Candy and milk chocolate

Drinks I Keep To A Minimum

>> Energy drinks
>> Commercial fruit juices
>> Alcohol – it's dehydrating BUT if I am feeling in a strong place with my skin, and the mood and company is right, I will treat myself to a glass of red wine, a gin and tonic or a glass of champagne

"Let food be thy medicine and medicine be thy food."

– Hippocrates

Healthy Gut

Our gut is often referred to as our second brain, it's so important to how well we function mentally. I learnt on my health coaching course that 70% of the immune system lives in the gut. Therefore, I do what I can to foster a healthy gut by maintaining a good balance of gut bacteria. I created most of these recipes with gut health in mind. Here are three key tips to get you started:

1 Eat from the list of foods that I embrace

2 Drink lots of fresh water with a slice of lemon – this is great for the liver too!

3 Consume both probiotics and prebiotics. Probiotics such as keifer, kombucha and kimchi introduce new good bacteria to the gut and prebiotics such as leeks, asparagus and chicory feed the good bacteria already present

"The key to living a happier, healthier life is inside us."

— Giulia Enders

Recipe Icons

All the recipes in this book have icons to show which foods are dairy-free, gluten-free, nightshade-free, paleo and vegan. The recipes were created out of love for the ingredients involved because they are delicious and nutritious, not out of fear or a need to 'ban' anything. However, we all know our own triggers so these icons are here to make life easier for you.

Dairy-Free

To be dairy-free is to avoid products containing milk. Dairy milk comes from mammals such as cattle, water buffaloes, goats, sheep and camels. Dairy products include food items such as yogurt, cheese and butter. You can find dairy-free plant based alternatives

Gluten-Free

A gluten-free diet is a diet that excludes the protein gluten. Gluten is found in grains such as wheat, barley, rye and a cross between wheat and rye called triticale. A gluten-free diet is essential for managing signs and symptoms of celiac disease and other medical conditions associated with gluten

Nightshade-Free

Nightshade vegetables form part of the Solanaceae plant family and include potatoes, peppers, tomatoes and aubergines (or eggplants)

Paleo

Paleo means anything that could be hunted or gathered before modern agriculture or food processing began, such as fish, seafood, lean meats, fruit, vegetables, nuts and seeds. Paleo followers avoid dairy, legumes and anything that has been processed or contains sugar

Vegan

Ingredients that don't use or contain animal products

Recipes for Glowing Skin

"One cannot think well, love well, sleep well, if one has not dined well."

— Virginia Woolf, A Room of One's Own

Hot Water with Fresh Mint & Lavender

" The greatest weath is health. "

Hot Water with Fresh Lemon

Prep/Cook Time: 3 mins

Serves: 1

3 x slices of lemon
1tbsp x raw honey (optional)

I absolutely love lemons. They bring back memories of my brother and I eating them raw when we were little – we absolutely loved the sour taste! Now I drink this every morning because I still love lemons, but I also learnt they are full of vitamin C and great for cleansing the liver. A healthy liver = healthy skin.

1. Place the lemon slices in a mug and pour over boiling water

2. Allow to infuse for a few minutes before stirring in the honey to taste

Fun Health Fact

Lemons are a great source of vitamin C, which is why early explorers took them on long voyages to avoid scurvy. Vitamin C is also needed to produce collagen, which we all know is great for glowing skin![7]

Hot Water with Ginger & Honey

Prep/Cook Time: 3 mins

Serves: 1

3-4 x thin slices of fresh ginger
        (unpeeled)
1tsp x raw honey

Picture this ... it's cold outside, you are snuggled up by the fire and you fancy a spicy, soothing kick to warm you up ... this is the go-to remedy!

1   Place the ginger in a mug and pour over boiling water

2   Allow to infuse for a few minutes before stirring in the honey to taste

Fun Health Fact

Honey is an ancient remedy for soothing cough and throat complaints, but it also has an ability to heal skin wounds. Its effectiveness lies in its levels of vitamins C, D, E K, and B complex, beta carotene, minerals, enzymes and essential oil.[1]

Hot Water with Fresh Mint & Lavender

Prep/Cook Time: 3 mins

Serves: 1

1 x sprig of fresh mint
1 x sprig of fresh lavender
or
1tsp x dried lavender

Every sip of this beautiful drink takes me back to the South of France. The taste and smell of fresh lavender and mint is so calming. If you want to soothe your mind and stomach, this is the cuppa for you.

1   Place the mint and lavender in a teapot or jug and pour over freshly boiled water

2   Allow to infuse for a few minutes before straining into a mug

Fun Health Fact:

Mint has antiseptic and anti-bacterial properties which soothe an upset stomach and relieve indigestion.[1]

Magical Warming Mylks

Prep/Cook Time: under 5 mins

Serves: 1

Luckily, almond, coconut, oatmeal, rice, cashew and other dairy-free milks are all readily available, healthy, nutritious and tasty. These magical warming mylks are a little cuddle in a glass and come in three different recipes that add fun, colour and flavour.

Chocolate:
250ml/1 cup x almond milk
1tbsp x raw cacao powder
1tbsp x maple syrup

Turmeric:
250ml/1 cup x cashew milk
1tsp x ground turmeric
1tbsp x raw honey
1tsp x ginger
Pinch of black pepper

Matcha:
250ml/1 cup x coconut milk
1tsp x matcha powder
2tbsp x boiling water
1tsp x maple syrup
Ice to serve

For chocolate and turmeric:

1 Assemble all the ingredients in a small pan

2 Heat over a low heat for 2-3mins, whisking well to combine

3 When steaming, pour into a mug

For The Matcha:

1 Mix the matcha powder, boiling water and maple syrup in a jug, whisking until combined and smooth

2 Fill a glass with ice and milk

3 Pour over the matcha mixture

Maple Latte

Serves: 1

1 x shot of espresso coffee
250ml/1 cup x almond milk
1-2tbsp x maple syrup to taste

This latte takes me straight back to some magical memories with my Canadian best friend. A maple latte is a cosier, healthier version of a caramel latte. Delish!

1 Place the almond milk and maple syrup in a pan and warm over a low heat. Whisk for 3-4mins until it simmers

2 Meanwhile make 1 shot of espresso in a mug

3 When the milk is steaming, pour over the espresso and stir together

Fun Health Fact:

Maple syrup is a healthier alternative to refined sugar. It has a distinctive, sweet, leafy flavour and is full of anti-bacterial properties and minerals such as manganese and zinc which heal and protect.[8]

Green Glow

Juices

"Looking after my body today gives me better HOPE for tomorrow."

— Anne Wilson Schael

Beautiful Blood Cleanser

Prep Time: 5 mins *Equipment:* Juicer

Serves: 2
(around 400ml/13½fl oz)

2 x beetroot
2 x pink lady apples
1 x lemon, juiced

I love the colour and earthy, sweet flavour of this juice. It is packed with skin glowing goodness and great before a workout.

1. Trim all the ingredients so they can fit through the juicer

2. Put through the juicer, stir and serve

Fun Health Fact
Beetroot is the boss! The pigments in beetroot, known as bioflavonoids, support the liver, improve circulation and purify our blood.[1]

Alkaline Me Up

Serves: 2
(around 400ml/13½fl oz)

2 x celery stalks
½ x cucumber
½ x broccoli head
100g/3½oz x asparagus stems
1 x lemon, juiced

As the name suggests, this is a juice full of greens which have an alkalising effect on the body. Research suggests disease can't survive in an alkaline state, so if you fancy an immune boost this is the juice for you.

1 Trim all the ingredients so they can fit through the juicer

2 Put through the juicer, stir and serve

Fun Health Fact

Celery is a veggie multi-tasker; it is rich in B vitamins and contains a great source of natural silicon and vitamin K, which are awesome for healthy skin and hair. It also helps to reduce stress.[1]

Vitamin A Booster

Serves: 2
(around 400ml/13½fl oz)

5 x medium carrots
1 x lemon, juiced
60g/2oz x fresh turmeric (optional)
1 inch x ginger
1 x apple (optional)

This bright orange drink brings sunshine to your table and is packed with skin glowing goodness! Add turmeric or ginger for an extra anti-inflammatory kick or add an apple if you prefer it a little sweeter, the choice is yours!

1 Trim all the ingredients so they can fit through the juicer

2 Put through the juicer, stir and serve

Fun Health Fact

Ginger's anti-inflammatory properties help soothe redness and irritation and protect your skin from pollution and UV rays. It also helps digestion AND boosts collagen which is great for glowing skin.[35]

Red Glow

Serves: 2
(around 400ml/13½fl oz)

½ x small watermelon, skin
      removed
25g/1oz x mint
1 x lime, juiced

This to me is a holiday in a glass. The combination of ingredients is so refreshing and always brings my mind to sunny days.

1 Trim all the ingredients so they can fit through the juicer

2 Put through the juicer, stir and serve

Fun Health Fact

The feather-light, pink-red flesh of a watermelon has many healing properties. This watery wonder is a good source of beta-carotene which converts to vitamin A – this keeps our immune system, eyes and skin healthy.[19]

Pink Glow

Prep Time: 5 mins Equipment: Juicer

Serves: 2
(around 400ml/13½fl oz)

½ x red cabbage
2 x pink lady apples
1 x lemon, juiced

Not only is this juice so aesthetically pleasing with it being pink, it's also a great contributor towards your daily fruit and vegetable intake!

1. Trim all the ingredients so they can fit through the juicer

2. Put through the juicer, stir and serve

Fun Health Fact

Heard the old proverb "an apple a day keeps the doctor away?" Well, apples are packed with minerals and antioxidants. Plus pectin extracted from apples may help to regulate gut bacteria, which helps inflammatory disorders.[13]

Green Glow

Prep Time: 5 mins *Equipment:* Juicer

Serves: 2
(around 400ml/13½fl oz)

½ x cucumber
2 x apples
2 x celery stalks
1 x lime, skin removed
25g/1oz (small piece) x ginger
    (optional)

A glowing green juice is an essential in my world. This is a juice I make on a regular basis due to the simplicity of the ingredients. Enjoy!

1 Trim all the ingredients so they can fit through the juicer

2 Put through the juicer, stir and serve

Fun Health Fact:

Cooling to both the taste and touch, cucumber acts as a natural 'cleanse and tone' as it helps to maintain water balance, and cleans and refreshes the intestines.[1]

Blue Lagoon Magic

"Nothing looks as good
as healthy feels."

Mint Choc Chip Protein Smoothie

Prep Time 5 mins *Equipment* Blender

Serves: 1
(around 350ml/1½ cups)

250ml/1 cup x hemp milk
Large handful of mint, leaves picked
1½ x frozen bananas
1 heaped tbsp x vanilla pea protein powder
1tsp x chlorella powder
1tsp x honey (optional)
1½tbsp x cacao nibs

A smoothie that brings me back to my happy days in California. It tastes just like mint choc chip but is full of skin glowing goodness!

1   Place all of the ingredients apart from the cacao nibs into the blender

2   Blend for 1-2 minutes until completely smooth

3   Add the cacao nibs and blitz slightly, still leaving crunchy nibs

4   Serve immediately

Fun Health Fact

A Japanese study showed that taking 4-6 grams of new algae on the block chlorella *before* consuming alcohol can prevent hangovers 96 percent of the time![2]

Acai Vibes

Prep Time: 5 mins *Equipment:* Blender

Serves: 1

Acai is a tropical, earthy, sweet berry. It's tasty, great for the skin and brings back superb memories of my travels to Bali and Australia.

For the smoothie:
1 x frozen banana
100g/3½oz x frozen mixed berries
1 x frozen sachet of acai berry
    puree
250ml/1 cup x dairy-free milk of
    choice

To serve:
Handful of berries (fresh or frozen)
Spoonful of nut butter
Handful of desiccated coconut

1   Put all the smoothie ingredients into the blender

2   Blend for 2-3minutes until smooth

3   Pour into a bowl and serve with chosen toppings

Fun Health Fact:

Acai is a little bluish, purple berry that originated in the Amazon rainforest of Brazil. It contains high levels of omegas 3, 6 and 9 as well as oleic acid, known to be a 'beautifying oil'.[21]

Tropical Green

Serves: 1

100ml/½ cup x coconut water
100ml/½ cup x pure aloe vera
    juice
25g/1oz x kale
Handful of mint, leaves picked
75g/2½oz x frozen mango

Tropical fruits are my favourite kind of fruits! This drink has a lovely kick of aloe vera too, which makes it cooling and cleansing. It works wonders for your skin!

1 Place all the ingredients into the blender

2 Blend for 1-2 minutes until completely smooth

3 Serve immediately

Fun Health Fact

Aloe vera is fierce! It contains polysaccharides which boost our immune systems and help fight a range of viral, fungal and bacterial infections.[2]

Chocolate Monkey

Prep Time: 5 mins *Equipment:* Blender

Serves: 1

Chocolate for breakfast? Yes please! A smoothie bowl full of chocolate, strawberries and crunchy granola. What's not to love?!

For the smoothie:
150ml/⅓ cup x almond milk
1½ x frozen bananas
1½tsp x raw cacao powder
1tbsp x vanilla pea protein powder
1tbsp x peanut butter or cashew
    butter (optional)
Sprinkle of sea salt

To serve:
Handful of chocolate granola
    (recipe on page 85)
Handful of strawberries, sliced
1tbsp x cacao nibs
½ x banana, sliced
½tsp x raw honey or maple syrup
    (optional)

1 Put all the smoothie ingredients into the blender

2 Blend for 1-2 minutes until completely smooth

3 Pour into a bowl and top with the optional toppings

Fun Health Fact:

Raw cacao contains tryptophan, a powerful, mood enhancing nutrient that helps reduce anxiety.[2]

Tropical Bliss

Prep Time: 5 mins *Equipment:* Blender

Serves: 1

This is my little bowl of tropical heaven. Every mouthful takes me to a sunnier place and I hope it does for you too.

For the smoothie:
60g/2oz x frozen mango
½ x frozen banana
60g/2oz x frozen pineapple
150ml/½ cup x coconut milk
1tbsp x vanilla pea protein powder

To serve:
Small handful of chia seeds
¼ x papaya, sliced
½ x kiwi, sliced
1 x passion fruit, seeds scooped

1 Place all the smoothie ingredients into the blender

2 Blend for 1-2 minutes until smooth

3 Place in a bowl and top with the sliced fruit

Fun Health Fact

Mangos are full of vitamin C and naturally boost the immune system. Papaya helps fight infections due to its antibacterial properties and is gentle and healing on the gut and stomach.[1]

Blue Lagoon Magic

Serves: 1

As the name suggests, it's mystical magic in a bowl. The blue colour is created from the superfood 'spirulina'. It's fun using natural powders to make food colourful. You can also use Pitaya powder as an alternative to make this recipe bright pink.

For The smoothie:
1tsp x blue spirulina
2 x frozen bananas
Splash of coconut milk

To serve:
Handful of coconut flakes
Handful of fresh blueberries

1. Put all the smoothie ingredients into the blender

2. Blend for 1-2 minutes until smooth

3. Place into a bowl and top with toppings

Fun Health Fact

This blue-green algae superfood is full of vitamin C and selenium, and it is also an excellent vegan source of iron.[17]

Grain-Free Bread

When it comes to quantity and eating between meals, I'm an advocate of whatever works best for you. Personally, I have three meals a day and a few snacks in between, but listen to your body and eat in a way that works best for you.

" Fall in love with taking care of your body."

Banana & Oat Bars

Prep Time: 5 mins *Cook Time:* 20 mins

Equipment: square baking tin approx 20cm x 20xm (8" x 8") lined with parchment paper

Makes: 12

This sweet and oaty combo makes energising bars for when you're on the go.

3 x ripe bananas
225g/3oz x gluten-free oats
75g x ground almonds
1-2tbsp x almond milk
1tsp x gluten-free baking powder
½tsp x cinnamon
2tbsp x maple syrup
1tbsp x almond butter
1tsp x salt

1   Preheat the oven to 180C/350F

2   Mash the bananas in a large mixing bowl then add the rest of the ingredients, mix well to combine

3   Pour the mixture into the prepared baking tin and smooth out the top. Bake for 15-18mins until golden on the top and slightly firm to touch

4   Remove and leave to cool for 10mins in the tray before taking out

5   Divide into 12 slices

Fun Health Fact:

Almonds are packed with magnesium and vitamins like B12, which make hair shiny and nails strong. They also contain naturally high levels of protein.[30]

Chocolate Bliss Balls

Prep Time: 5 mins Cook Time: 20 mins Equipment: Food processor, baking sheet and parchment paper

Makes: 12
(35g/1¼oz balls)

150g/5¼oz x hazelnuts
8 x medjool dates, pitted
1tbsp x peanut butter or cashew
    butter
3tbsp x raw cacao powder
1tbsp x maple syrup or raw honey
Pinch of sea salt
1tbsp x desiccated coconut

For Topping:
3tbsp x desiccated coconut

I adore raw chocolate and I'm fascinated by the health benefits that are good for our skin. Mix these up, roll them, pop them in the fridge and enjoy. They really are that simple to make.

1 Put the hazelnuts into a food processor and pulse for 1 minute, until they resemble breadcrumbs

2 Add in all the other ingredients and pulse until the mixture comes together

3 Line a baking sheet with parchment paper then divide and roll mixture into balls, each the size of a large walnut (about 35g/1¼oz)

4 Once they are shaped, fill a small dish with the extra desiccated coconut and roll each ball in the coconut until completely coated

5 Place on the baking sheet and leave to set in the freezer for at least 20mins

Fun Health Fact

One of the "fruits of paradise" in Islamic tradition, dates can be used for everything from omelettes to dips and are super nutritious too.[32]

Hummus & Veggie Sticks

Prep Time 5 mins Cook Time 5 mins Equipment Food processor

Makes: 500g/17½oz of each

Who doesn't love a dip and nibble with friends? Super easy to make, these three-coloured, flavoured hummus and veggie sticks are fun to look at, tasty to eat and great for sharing. The additional flavours like basil really adds an edge and I sometimes garnish with edible flowers for a little wow factor.

Beetroot hummus:
2 x cooked, peeled beetroot
1 x 400g/13½oz tinned chickpeas
2tbsp x tahini
4tbsp x olive oil
½ x lemon, squeezed
1tsp x salt
1tsp x nigella seeds

Turmeric hummus:
1 x 400g/13½oz tinned chickpeas
2tbsp x tahini
4tbsp x hemp oil
½ x lemon, squeezed
1tsp x turmeric
1tsp x salt
1tsp x chilli flakes

Basil hummus:
25g/1oz x basil
1 x 400g/13½oz tinned chickpeas
2tbsp x tahini
4tbsp x avocado oil
½ x lemon squeezed
1tsp x salt
1tsp x sesame seeds

To serve
Celery, cucumber and carrots

For the beetroot hummus:
1. Place all the ingredients except for the nigella seeds in a food processor and blitz to a rough textured paste – add a little water if the mixture is too thick. Check seasoning and blitz again

2. Lightly toast the nigella seeds and stir through the hummus

For the Turmeric hummus:
1. Place all the ingredients except for the chilli flakes in a food processor and blitz to a rough textured paste – add a little water if the mixture is too thick. Check seasoning and blitz again

2. Sprinkle over the chilli flakes

For the basil hummus:
1. Place all the ingredients except for the sesame seeds in a food processor and blitz to a rough textured paste – add a little water if the mixture is too thick. Check seasoning and blitz again

2. Lightly toast the sesame seeds and stir through the hummus

Avocado on Oatcakes

Prep/Cook Time: 5 mins

Serves: 2

1 x avocado
Squeeze of lemon
Handful of chives, chopped
Sea salt
4 x gluten-free oat or rice cakes

This snack is so quick to make; mash it, add a few fresh chives, a squeeze of lemon and you are done. A refreshing, tasty snack that is perfect for eating on the go.

1   Scoop the avocado into a bowl and roughly mash with a fork, then season with a squeeze of lemon juice and salt before stirring through the chopped chives

2   Spoon on top of the oatcakes

Fun Health Fact

Loaded with healthy fats, the flesh and oil of avocados are anti-inflammatory and contain anti-oxidants and omega-3 fatty acids, which help lubricate the joints.[1]

Grain-Free Bread

Makes: 1 small loaf

300g/3 cups x almond flour
60g/½ cup x coconut flour
40g/½ cup x milled flaxseed
40g/½ cup x milled psyllium husk
30g/2tbsp x flaxseed
30g/2tbsp x sunflower seeds
1tbsp x baking powder
1tsp x salt
3tbsp x olive oil
2tsp x raw cider vinegar
400ml/1½ cups x water
Handful of quinoa flakes
Handful of flaxseed

For Turmeric Coconut oil
2tsp x coconut oil
A pinch of turmeric

I find minimising grains works best for me, though you'll notice I still keep them in other recipes. This grain-free bread is perfect for on the go – throw it in the toaster, pop some 'tumeric coconut oil' on top, and you have a warm, filling snack that is so easy to prepare. Make it in advance, freeze it and then defrost slice by slice, as and when.

1   Preheat the oven to 220C/430F

2   Place the almond flour, coconut flour, milled flaxseed, psyllium husk, flaxseed, sunflower seeds, baking powder and salt in a large bowl and mix together well

3   Add the olive oil, vinegar and water then stir until it begins to form a dough

4   Bring together with wet hands, knead briefly and shape into a long round loaf

5   Place in the prepared tin and sprinkle over the handfuls of quinoa flakes and flaxseed, gently pressing them into the surface

6   Bake for 20mins until the crust is firm and golden then turn the oven down to 180C/350F and bake for a further 30-40mins until a skewer inserted into the middle comes out clean

7   Leave until completely cooled before slicing

Homemade Coconut Yogurt with Berries

Prep Time: 5 mins Setting Time: 12 hrs

Makes: 800ml/1½pt

400ml/13½fl oz x coconut cream
2tbsp x maple syrup
4 x probiotic capsules

To serve:
Handful of raspberries
Drizzle of maple syrup

I love coconuts and this delicious snack is a favourite of mine. I hope you enjoy it as much as I do.

1 Stir the coconut cream and maple syrup together in a bowl

2 Twist open the probiotic capsules, add the powder to the cream and stir again

3 Leave uncovered in a warm place for 4-6hrs then transfer to a sterilised jar, cover and place in the fridge for a further 6hrs to finish setting

4 Serve with the fresh berries and a swirl of maple syrup

Fun Health Fact

Raspberries, known as 'nature's candy' are rich in colour, sweet, juicy and high in nutrients and ellagic acid, which has anti-inflammatory properties.[12]

Seeded Teff Crackers

Prep Time 5 mins *Cook Time* 14 mins *Equipment* 2 x large sheets of parchment paper

Makes: a large baking sheet's worth of crackers

A super quick nutritious snack that is delicious and perfect served warm with homemade hummus dip (recipe found on page 63).

80g/¾ cup x teff flour
60g/½ cup x buckwheat flour
50ml/3½tbsp x olive oil
6tbsp x boiling water
Pinch of sea salt
1tbsp x sunflower seeds
1tbsp x pumpkin seeds
1tsp x sea salt

1. Preheat the oven to 190C/375F

2. Put the teff and buckwheat flour into a bowl, add a pinch of sea salt and pour in the olive oil. Rub between finger tips until it begins to come together into a crumble consistency

3. Stir in the boiling water and then gently knead with your hands until the dough is moist and sticks together

4. Form into a flat circle on a piece of baking parchment and cover with another large sheet of parchment. Roll the dough between the sheets of parchment until it is about 1½mm/0.05" thick. Peel off the top layer of parchment paper

5. Sprinkle over the seeds and sea salt, pressing firmly into the dough

6. Bake for 12-14mins until golden and firm to touch

7. Leave to cool for 10mins before breaking into crackers

Fun Health Fact

Along with being gluten-free, high in iron and super tasty, the tiny grain teff has also recently been called Hollywood's new superfood and the new quinoa.[6]

Avocado & Salmon on Toast

"I really regret eating well today... said no one ever."

Pink & Green Quinoa Bowl

Sauerkraut Prep Time: 15 mins Ferment Time: 5 days-2 weeks Prep/Cook Time: 5 mins

Serves: 2

You know those days when you wake up hungry or you've had an early session in the gym and only a big breakfast will do? That's a quinoa bowl day. It's earthy, energising and packed with protein. I like salmon in mine but an alternative is to try it with chickpeas.

For the quinoa bowl:
200g/2 cups x wholegrain quinoa, cooked
1 x large spoonful beetroot hummus (see page 63)
1 x large spoonful sauerkraut
50g/1½oz x smoked salmon or 50g/1½oz tinned chickpeas
Large handful of spinach
1 x avocado, sliced
8 x radishes, finely sliced
2tbsp x olive oil
1tbsp x nigella seeds
Small handful fresh dill, roughly chopped

Small handful fresh mint leaves, roughly chopped

For the sauerkraut:
1 x white cabbage (about 1½kg, finely shredded)
6tbsp x Himalayan sea salt
1tbsp x juniper berries

To make the quinoa bowl

1 Place the quinoa in the bottom of a large bowl with a spoonful of sauerkraut (see below) and hummus in the centre

2 Arrange the salmon, or chickpeas and vegetables around this, scatter over the nigella seeds and fresh herbs then drizzle over the olive oil

To make the sauerkraut

1 Combine the cabbage and salt in a large bowl and massage with your hands for 10mins. Slowly the cabbage will begin to release liquid

2 Add the juniper berries and transfer to a large sterilised jar or container. Cover loosely with cling film and place a plate on top to ensure that the cabbage is immersed in the liquid

3 Leave in a cool dark place (about 18-20C) for at least 5 days to allow the cabbage to begin to ferment. It takes around 2 weeks for the flavour to fully develop. Once it is to your liking, transfer to a smaller sterilised jar and keep in the fridge for up to 6 months

Gluten-Free Porridge

Serves: 2

A comforting bowl of oats in three different flavours, perfect all year round. It's a healthy pudding option too. This will keep you going all morning.

100g/1 cup x gluten-free porridge oats
200-250ml/7-8fl oz x almond milk

Chocolate:
2tbsp x raw cacao powder
1 x banana, sliced to serve
1tbsp x maple syrup to serve

Raspberry:
1tbsp x Pitaya powder
Handful of fresh raspberries to serve

Vanilla:
1tbsp x vanilla pea protein powder
2tbsp x almond butter to serve

1 Place the oats and milk into a pan and heat gently, stirring all the time. Mix in your chosen flavour and gently bubble for 10mins until the porridge is thick and creamy, adding a little more milk if necessary

2 Serve with your chosen toppings

Fun Health Fact:

Oats contain alkaloid gamine, a natural sedative which can treat depression, anxiety, and insomnia.[1]

Grain-Free Banana Bread

Prep Time: 10 mins *Cook Time:* 50 mins

Equipment: 450g/1lb loaf tin approx 22cm x 12cm (8" x 4") lined with parchment paper

Makes: 1 small loaf

- 4 x medium ripe bananas, 3 for the batter and 1 reserved for the top
- 220g/2 cups x chestnut flour, sifted
- ½tbsp x ground cinnamon
- 1tbsp x mixed spice
- 1tsp x gluten-free baking powder
- ½tsp x bicarbonate of soda/ baking soda
- Pinch of sea salt
- 150ml/¾ cup x coconut oil
- ½ x lemon, juiced
- 90g/½ cup x coconut yogurt
- 100g/½ cup x tahini
- 50g/4tbsp x raw honey

I'm bananas about bananas! This grain-free banana bread is a perfect breakfast for on the go. Make this in advance, store it in the freezer and defrost it slice by slice! Enjoy with a healthy spread of nut butter.

1. Preheat oven to 180C/350F

2. In a bowl mash together 3 of the bananas with a pinch of salt. In another bowl sift the flour, baking powder, bicarbonate of soda and all the spices together

3. In a third bowl mix together the tahini, coconut yoghurt, coconut oil, lemon juice and honey. Add the mashed banana and whisk until the mixture is smooth and glossy

4. Gently fold the dry ingredients into the banana and tahini mixture

5. Pour into the prepared loaf tin and smooth out the top. Slice the reserved banana in half lengthways and place on top of the mixture

6. Place tin in the middle of the oven for 45-50mins or until golden and a skewer inserted in the middle comes out clean

7. Leave to cool in the tin for 10mins then turn out and leave to cool on a wire rack

Fun Health Fact:

Bananas are rich in potassium and act as natural antacids which soothe the tummy. They also contain slow release sugars that are great for busy people on the go.[1]

Chia Seed Pudding

Prep Time: 5 mins Cook Time: 4 hrs or overnight

Serves: 2

30g/½ cup x chia seeds
200ml/7fl oz x almond milk
2tbsp x maple syrup or raw honey
  (optional)

Chocolate:
1tbsp x raw cacao powder

To serve:
1tsp x cacao nibs
1 x sliced banana
2tbsp x maple syrup or raw honey
  (optional)

Raspberry:
2tsp x Pitaya powder

To serve:
Handful of raspberries
Handful of pink edible flowers,
  (see page 143)
2tbsp x maple syrup or raw honey
  (optional)

Vanilla:
2tsp x vanilla pea protein powder

To serve:
Handful of coconut flakes
Handful of goji berries
2tbsp x maple syrup or raw honey
  (optional)

This is super easy, super fun and super nutritious! Prepare this the night before and it's like having pudding for breakfast. Mix the chia seeds, milk and your flavour of choice, leave overnight, wake up and enjoy!

1 Mix the chia seeds, almond milk and optional maple syrup or raw honey together in a bowl then add the cacao, Pitaya or vanilla depending on which you are using. Whisk well to ensure everything is incorporated

2 Cover and leave in the fridge for a minimum of 4hrs or overnight

3 Serve with your chosen toppings

Fun Health Fact

The gum-like fibre in chia seeds promotes bowel regularity and stabilises blood sugar.[1]

Avocado & Salmon on Toast

Prep/Cook Time 5 mins

Serves: 2

2 x slices of grain-free bread
(recipe found on page 67)
1 x ripe avocado, sliced
50g/1½oz x smoked salmon or
50g/1½oz cooked shiitake
mushrooms
Small handful of flaxseed
Small handful of sunflower seeds
Squeeze of lemon
Drizzle of hemp oil
Freshly ground black pepper

A classic breakfast or brunch – gorgeous mashed avocado and delicious fresh salmon on grain-free bread. The sprinkle of sunflower seeds and flaxseed adds a crunchy texture and the omegas are good for your skin. If you are vegan, try swapping the salmon for shiitake mushrooms.

1. Toast the bread then place the avocado and the salmon or shiitake mushrooms on top

2. Scatter over the seeds and finish with a squeeze of lemon, a drizzle of hemp oil and lots of freshly ground pepper

Fun Health Fact

Ground flaxseed is packed with protein, fibre, omega-3 fatty acids, vitamins and minerals.[24]

Fun Health Fact

To make your granola last longer, preserve it in an airtight container and it will stay fresh for up to two weeks.

Grain & Nut-Free Chocolate Granola

Prep Time: 5 mins Cook Time: 10 mins Equipment: Baking tin lined with parchment paper

Serves: 2

60g/1 cup x coconut flakes
50g/1 cup x quinoa flakes
50g/1 cup x flaxseed
50g/1 cup x chia seeds
3tbsp x maple syrup
2tbsp x raw cacao powder
30g/1 cup x buckwheat puffs or
    puffed rice
100g/3½oz x medjool dates,
    chopped

To serve

Coconut yogurt to serve (recipe
    found on page 69)
Fresh berries to serve

Another grain-free breakfast recipe (if using the buckwheat puffs). A crunchy, energising bowl of goodness. Perfect when topped with coconut yogurt, or a fantastic addition to smoothie bowls.

1 Preheat the oven to 180C/350F. Mix ¾ of the coconut flakes with all the quinoa flakes, flaxseed, chia seeds, maple syrup and cacao together in a bowl

2 Spread on the lined baking tin

3 Bake for 5mins until beginning to crisp then mix again and return to the oven for a further 5mins

4 Leave to cool then stir through the dates, buckwheat puffs and remaining coconut flakes

5 Serve with the coconut yogurt and fresh berries

Seabass with Cauliflower & Fennel

"For happy health, fuel yourself
with dreams and greens."

— Terri Guillemets

Prawn Salad

Prep/Cook Time: 5 mins

Serves: 2

175g/6oz x cooked king prawns or
   another choice of seafood
1 x avocado, sliced
100g/3½oz x baby spinach
1 x courgette/zucchini, peeled into
   ribbons
Pinch of chilli flakes
½ x lemon, squeezed
2tbsp x olive oil
Handful of fresh basil, roughly
   chopped
Handful of fresh parsley, roughly
   chopped
Sea salt
Pepper

I love the Mediterranean way of eating. Fresh seafood, lots of vegetables and maybe the odd glass of organic wine. This salad is super fresh and full of herby flavours. Divine!

1   Place the prawns, avocado, spinach and courgette/zucchini in a large bowl, sprinkle over the chilli flakes, lemon juice and olive oil and toss together

2   Season with salt and pepper to taste, toss again and serve with the herbs scattered over

Fun Health Fact:

Pick fresh basil leaves from their stalks and scatter whole, or roughly torn, over dishes for a sweet undertone.[11]

Fun Health Fact

Broccoli is brimming with detoxifying and anti-inflammatory ingredients, but it's also packed with glucosinolate compounds, such as sulforaphane and glucoraphanin, which help to fight cancer.[33]

Buckwheat Noodle Buddha Bowl

Prep Time: 10 mins *Cook Time:* 20 mins *Equipment:* Roasting tray

Serves: 2

A beautiful bowl of earthy goodness with tropical smells and flavours. I love throwing this meal together – it always makes me smile.

1 x chicken breast (optional)
100g/3½oz x buckwheat soba noodles
1tbsp x virgin sesame oil
100g/3½oz x edamame beans
100g/3½oz x tenderstem broccoli, sliced in half lengthways
2tbsp x tahini
2tbsp x tamari
2tbsp x rice wine vinegar
6 x spring onions, finely sliced
¼ x cucumber, finely sliced
6 x radishes, finely sliced
1tbsp x sesame seeds
Handful of nasturtium leaves and flowers
Handful of chopped coriander

1. Preheat the oven to 200C/390F. Place the chicken breast on a roasting tray and cook for 10-12mins until the juices run clear. Remove from the oven and leave to cool

2. Bring a large pan of water to the boil and cook the noodles for 8-10mins until tender. Drain and refresh briefly under cold water, drain well and toss with a drizzle of sesame oil

3. Blanch the edamame beans and broccoli in boiling water for 2-3mins then drain

4. Whisk together the tahini, rice wine vinegar, tamari and sesame oil to make the dressing

5. Assemble all the ingredients in a bowl, drizzle over the dressing and scatter over the sesame seeds, herbs and flowers

Smoked Salmon Courgetti

Prep Time 5 mins *Cook Time* 5 mins *Equipment* Julienne peeler or spiraliser

Serves: 2

2 x courgettes/zucchini
1tbsp x olive oil
100g/3½oz x smoked salmon, sliced
Handful of chives, roughly chopped
1tbsp x salted capers
¼ x lemon, juiced
Black pepper

Minimal ingredients necessary, yet so beautiful and delicious. A winner all round when cooking for friends. Top tip – if you want a creamier version, try adding dairy-free cheese.

1 Using a spiraliser or julienne peeler create thin ribbons of courgette/ zucchini spaghetti

2 Warm the olive oil in a large frying pan over a low heat, add the courgetti and toss briefly for 2mins until just cooked

3 Remove from the heat, add the smoked salmon, chives and capers, then toss together

4 Squeeze over the lemon juice and season with black pepper

Fun Health Fact

Courgette is a brilliant internal cleanser with its phytonutrients that promote bowel regularity and aid water balance. It also contains high levels of vitamin C and potassium.[1]

Baked Sweet Potatoes with Baked Beans & Slaw

Prep Time: 20 mins Cook Time: 1 hr Equipment: Baking tray

Serves: 2

My healthy take on the jacket potato. This traybake is super easy to do and the slaw gives it a lovely chilli, crunchy kick.

2 x sweet potatoes, scrubbed

For The beans:
2tbsp x olive oil
1 x onion, finely sliced
2 x garlic cloves, finely sliced
1tsp x ground cumin
1tsp x ground coriander
2 x 400g/13½oz tins black beans,
    drained and rinsed
150ml/5fl oz x water
1tsp x smoked sea salt
1 x lime, juiced
Handful of fresh coriander,
    chopped

For The slaw:
½ x red onion, finely sliced
1 x raw beetroot, coarsely grated
2 x carrots, coarsely grated
1 x green chilli, finely chopped
1 x small bunch fresh coriander,
    roughly chopped
1 x lime, juiced
2tbsp x olive oil
Sea salt
Pepper

1. Preheat the oven to 200C/390F. Place the sweet potatoes on a baking tray, sprinkle with salt and bake for 1hr

2. Make the beans while the potatoes are cooking. Heat the oil in a pan and gently fry the onion and garlic over a medium heat for 5-7mins

3. Stir in the cumin and ground coriander then cook for another 2mins before adding the beans, water and salt. Stir well and bring to a simmer for 10-12mins, stirring frequently until the beans have broken apart and are thick and creamy

4. Squeeze over the fresh lime juice and stir in the chopped coriander

5. Make the slaw while the beans are cooking. Mix all the ingredients together in a bowl and season to taste

6. When the sweet potatoes have crispy skin and soft flesh take them from the oven. Split them open and top with the beans and slaw and an extra sprinkling of smoked sea salt

Seabass with Cauliflower & Fennel

Prep Time: 10 mins **Cook Time:** 25 min **Equipment:** Baking tray

Serves: 2

2 x fresh seabass fillets
½ x cauliflower, divided into small florets
2 x fennel bulbs, sliced into wedges
½ x lemon, zest and squeezed juice
1tbsp x za'atar
2tbsp x olive oil
Handful of pumpkin seeds
50g/2oz x black olives, pitted
1 x small bunch parsley, roughly chopped
Lemon wedges, to serve
Sea salt
Pepper

Seabass is one of my favourite dishes – it's tasty, light and easy to make. Cauliflower and fennel are super veggies and packed full of nutrients, delicious on the side.

1. Preheat the oven to 200C/390F. Spread the cauliflower and fennel onto a baking tray and drizzle with olive oil, lemon zest and juice and za'atar. Roast in the oven for 12mins until they begin to crisp and are nearly cooked

2. Remove from the oven and sprinkle over the pumpkin seeds and olives. Nestle the seabass fillets in between the cauliflower and fennel and drizzle with a little more oil

3. Bake for a further 8-10mins until the seabass is just beginning to flake. Sprinkle over the freshly chopped parsley, season with salt and pepper, and serve immediately with lemon wedges

Fun Health Fact:

Fennel has a triple whammy of healing properties – it soothes digestion, relieves water retention and regulates female hormones.[1]

Crispy Haddock with Mint Potatoes

Prep Time 5 mins *Cook Time* 20 mins

Serves: 2

400g/14oz x new potatoes
2 x skinless haddock fillets (approx 175g each)
30g/⅓ cup x buckwheat flour
5tbsp x olive oil
100g/3½oz x peas
A few sprigs of fresh mint, leaves picked and roughly chopped
A few sprigs of fresh parsley, roughly chopped
¼ x lemon, squeezed
Sea salt
Pepper

A few tweaks can go a long way. I use buckwheat flour to give the fish a crispy skin and crush the potatoes with peas and mint to make the flavours pop.

1. Bring the potatoes to the boil in a pan of water then cook for 12-15mins until tender

2. While the potatoes are cooking, place the flour on a plate and season with salt and pepper. Toss the haddock fillets in the flour, shaking off any excess. Heat 3tbsps of the oil in a frying pan over a medium heat then fry the haddock for 2½-3mins on each side until brown and crispy

3. Once the potatoes are cooked, blanch the peas in boiling water and drain. Drain the potatoes, combine them with the peas and lightly crush them with a fork. Squeeze over the lemon juice, drizzle the remaining olive oil and scatter over the mint. Toss together, season with salt and pepper and serve with the haddock

Fun Health Fact

Peas are rich in vitamin K, manganese and vitamin C and are great for the gut.[22]

Pad Thai

"I have chosen to be happy because it is good for my health."

— Voltaire

Comforting Cottage Pie

Prep Time: 20 mins Cook Time: 1 hr 30 mins Equipment: Ovenproof dish approx 20cm x 15cm (7.8" x 5.9")

Serves: 2

This is a favourite childhood meal, adapted with turkey and sweet potatoes. My friends and family love this dish!

3 small or 2 large x sweet potatoes, scrubbed
1 x onion, finely sliced
1 x leek, finely sliced
2 x carrots, finely diced
2 x garlic cloves, finely sliced
4 x sprigs of fresh thyme, leaves picked
3 x anchovy fillets
400g/14oz x turkey mince
2tbsp x chestnut flour
300ml/10fl oz x chicken bone broth or vegetable stock
4tbsp x olive oil
Sea salt
Pepper

To serve
1 cup x peas
Sea salt
1 x sprig of fresh mint

1 Preheat the oven to 180C/350F

2 Place the sweet potatoes in a roasting tray and roast in the oven for 1hr until the insides are soft

3 While the sweet potatoes are cooking, heat 2tbsp of the olive oil in a large deep frying pan and sauté the onion, leek, carrots and garlic over a low heat for 12-15mins until golden and translucent

4 Add the thyme and anchovies and cook these for another 2mins, stirring well

5 Add the turkey mince and cook on a high heat, stirring often for 5-7mins until well browned

6 Add the flour and stock, season with salt and pepper and bubble over a low heat for 5mins

7 Once the sweet potatoes are cool enough to handle, peel away the skin and mash the flesh with a fork then add the remaining olive oil and season to taste

8 Place the filling into the ovenproof dish and top with the mash

9 Bake at 180C/350F for 30-35mins until bubbling and starting to brown on top

Dinner   103

Thai Green Curry

Prep Time 20 mins *Cook Time* 20 mins *Equipment* Blender

Serves: 2

A spicy kick, full of flavour and skin glowing goodness.

For the curry paste:
6 x spring onions, trimmed and roughly chopped
2 x garlic cloves, roughly chopped
1 x thumb-sized piece of ginger, unpeeled and roughly chopped
2 x green chillies, roughly chopped
1 x fresh lemongrass stalk, roughly chopped
2 x kaffir lime leaves
1tsp x ground coriander
1 x bunch fresh coriander with stalks, roughly chopped
1tbsp x tamari
1 x lime, juiced
Splash of water

For the curry:
1tbsp x coconut oil
200g/7oz x butternut squash (about half), peeled and cut into 2cm/¾" cubes
400ml/13½fl oz x coconut milk
100g/3½oz x green beans, trimmed
100g/3½oz x baby spinach
2tbsp x fish sauce
200g/7oz x raw king prawns
Squeeze of lime
1 x bunch Thai basil, torn
1 x red chilli, finely sliced (optional)

To serve
200g/7oz x cooked quinoa

1. Place all the ingredients for the curry paste into a blender and blitz until you have a rough paste, adding a little water if it is too dry to blend

2. Heat the oil in a large pan and add the curry paste, stirring frequently over a medium heat for 2-3mins until the paste looks dry and smells fragrant. Watch it closely making sure it doesn't burn and become bitter

3. Add the butternut squash and the coconut milk and stir well to combine. Bring to the boil, cover and simmer gently for 7-8mins, stirring occasionally until the squash begins to soften

4. Add the fish sauce followed by the prawns and beans, mix well, cover again and cook for 3-4 mins until the beans are tender and the prawns are pink

5. Add the spinach and stir though until it is just wilted

6. Season with a bit more lime juice and scatter over the Thai basil. Scatter over a few chillies if you like a bit more of a kick. Serve with cooked quinoa

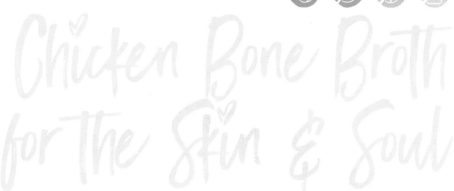

Chicken Bone Broth for the Skin & Soul

Prep Time: 10 mins Cook Time: 4-8 hrs Equipment: Ovenproof pan or slow cooker

Serves: 2

They say 'chicken soup is good for the soul' and I agree. This recipe is full of bone broth goodness, which supports in healing your gut.

For the broth:
500g/17½oz x bone-in chicken pieces e.g. thighs/drumsticks/wings
1 x onion, roughly chopped
2 x celery stalks, roughly chopped
2 x carrots, peeled and chopped into large chunks
2 x parsnips, peeled and chopped into large chunks
5 x sprigs of fresh thyme
1 x bay leaf
1tbsp x turmeric
1tbsp x peppercorns
2tbsp x raw cider vinegar
1tsp x sea salt

To serve:
1 x small bunch parsley, roughly chopped
Squeeze of lemon
Pepper
Sea salt

1 Place all the ingredients into an ovenproof pan or slow cooker so they are tightly packed in then cover completely in water

2 If using a slow cooker, set to low and cook for 6-8hrs

3 Otherwise preheat the oven to 130C/260F. Bring the pan to the boil, then transfer to the oven for 4-5hrs

4 Once cooked, remove the chicken and shred the meat, discarding the bones

5 Return the meat to the pan and stir through the chopped parsley

6 Season with a squeeze of lemon and salt and pepper to taste

Pad Thai

Prep Time: 10 mins Cook Time: 12 mins Equipment: Wok

Serves: 2

This flavoursome dish is Thailand in a bowl. It's based on the classic pad thai and is packed full of spices, tangy tastes and textures.

150g/5oz x flat brown rice noodles
3tbsp x coconut oil
6 x spring onions, finely sliced
100g/3½oz x mangetout or sugar snap peas, finely sliced
100g/3½oz x chinese cabbage, finely shredded
2 x carrots, finely shredded
100g/3½oz x bean sprouts
2tbsp x fish sauce
2tbsp x tamari
3tbsp x rice wine
1 x lime, juiced
1 x red chilli, finely sliced (optional)
Handful of roasted peanuts, roughly chopped (optional)
1 x small bunch coriander

1 Bring a large pan of water to the boil and cook the noodles for 10mins. Drain and refresh briefly under cold water then drain well and toss in a little oil

2 In a small bowl whisk together the fish sauce, tamari, rice wine and lime juice to make the dressing

3 Heat the rest of the oil in a wok or large frying pan and stir-fry the spring onions, mangetout, cabbage and carrots over a high heat for 1min until just beginning to wilt, then add the beansprouts and cook for a further 30secs

4 Add the dressing to the wok, allow to bubble briefly then add the noodles and toss well to combine

5 Serve with a sprinkling of peanuts, coriander, chilli and another squeeze of lime

Fun Health Fact

Coriander is not only great for lowering cholesterol but it is also a super tasty addition to curries and stir-frys and a great scent for yogurts and marinades.[25]

Green Glowing Goddess Soup

Prep Time: 10 mins Cook Time: 10 mins Equipment: Hand blender

Serves: 2

1 x onion, finely sliced
1 x leek, finely sliced
2tbsp x olive oil
300ml/10fl oz x vegetable stock
100g/3½oz x peas
1 x bunch watercress (about 100g)
150ml/3½fl oz x almond milk
Handful of pumpkin seeds
Sea salt
Pepper

To serve
Olive oil,
2 x slices grain-free bread to serve
    (recipe found on page 67)

A vegetarian and vegan friendly broth full of light veggies to get you glowing inside and out.

1. In a large saucepan heat the olive oil and gently fry the onion and leek over a very gentle heat for 5-7mins until soft and translucent

2. Add the vegetable stock and bring to the boil then add the peas and boil briefly for 2mins

3. Remove from the heat then add the watercress and almond milk and blitz with a hand blender until smooth

4. Return to the pan and heat gently without allowing the soup to boil, season with salt and pepper to taste

5. Gently toast the pumpkin seeds in a dry frying pan, watching them closely so they do not burn

6. Serve the soup with the toasted seeds scattered on top, a drizzle of oil and the grain-free bread

Fun Health Fact

The powerhouse cousin of kale, watercress fights many chronic diseases including cancer. It's packed with phytonutrients that our bodies thrive on, meaning great hair, nails and teeth too.[10]

Steak & Chips

Serves: 2

2 x grass-fed fillet steaks (about 200g/7oz each, 2½cm/1" thick) or cauliflower sliced into '2 large steaks'
2 x sweet potatoes, scrubbed and sliced into wedges
150g/5oz x asparagus spears, trimmed
2tbsp x coconut oil
Sea salt
Pepper

For the chimichurri:
3 x spring onions, roughly chopped
2 x garlic cloves, roughly chopped
1 x green chilli, roughly chopped (optional)
6tbsp x olive oil
½ x lime, juiced
1 x small bunch fresh coriander
1 x small bunch fresh parsley
Sea salt

A classic, hearty meal and a popular choice for some. Personally, I'm conscious of the amount of meat I eat, so when I do, I ensure it is organic and grass-fed. For a vegan alternative you can replace the steak with cauliflower which I have also shared how to make. Enjoy!

1. To make the chimichurri place all the ingredients into the food processor and blitz to form a rough puree

2. Remove the steak from the fridge an hour before you are ready to cook to bring to room temperature. Rub with olive oil and season generously with black pepper on both sides

3. Preheat the oven to 200C/375F. Place the sweet potato wedges on a roasting tray, toss in the oil and season with a little salt and pepper

4. Bake for 30mins in total, but after 20mins add the asparagus, toss in the oil and return to the oven

5. As soon as you've added the asparagus, begin to cook your steak. Heat a griddle pan until smoking hot and add the steaks. Cook them for 2-3mins on each side for rare, 3-4mins for medium and 4-5mins for well done

6. If you are using the cauliflower, brush the 'steaks' with a little olive oil and cook for 3mins on each side until tender

7. Rest the steaks for 2mins, remove the vegetables from the oven and serve with the chimichurri

Matcha Lime Cheesecake

"Your body holds deep wisdom. Trust in it. Learn from it. Nourish it."

— Bella Bleue

Nice Cream

Prep Time: 5 mins *Equipment:* Food processor

Serves: 2

Strawberry:
2 x frozen bananas
75g/1 cup x frozen strawberries
1tsp x vanilla pea protein powder
Splash of dairy-free milk

Vanilla:
3 x frozen bananas
2tsp x vanilla extract
1tbsp x vanilla pea protein powder
Splash of dairy-free milk

Chocolate:
3 x frozen bananas
1tbsp x raw cacao powder
1tsp x vanilla pea protein powder
Splash of dairy-free milk

This is so simple; it's literally frozen bananas, a dash of dairy-free milk and you've basically got healthy ice cream. Make it for yourself, make it for friends, tuck in, relax and feel good! Perfect for the summer months!

1 Place all the ingredients into a food processor and blitz on high speed for about 30secs until smooth

2 Eat immediately

Fun Health Fact

Bananas help regulate the heart function and blood pressure plus the resistant starch inside them has a prebiotic effect, which helps keep the gut happy.[1]

Banana Pancakes

Prep Time: 10 mins *Cook Time:* 10 mins *Equipment:* Food processor

Serves: 2 / Makes 8

100g/3½oz x gluten-free oats
2 x bananas
50g/1¾oz x buckwheat flour
50g/1¾oz x ground almonds
1tbsp x milled flaxseed
1 heaped tsp x gluten-free baking
    powder
125ml/4¼fl oz x almond milk
Pinch of sea salt
1tbsp x raw honey or maple syrup
2-3tbsp x coconut oil

To serve:
Spoonful of coconut yogurt
Handful of blueberries
Drizzle of maple syrup

These pancakes are a fun recipe that gets everyone involved. Who doesn't love flipping pancakes? Top with your favourite treats – I love mine with coconut yogurt and blueberries!

1   Place the oats into a food processor and blend into a powder

2   Add the rest of the ingredients apart from the coconut oil and briefly pulse until the mixture comes together

3   Heat the coconut oil in a large frying pan over a gentle heat. Add a few scoops of the batter (around 2tbsp per pancake) and cook over a gentle heat for 2-3 mins. Very carefully flip the pancake and cook on the other side for the same amount of time

4   Keep covered on a warm plate until all of the pancakes are ready

5   Serve with coconut yogurt (recipe found on page 69), blueberries and maple syrup drizzled over the top

Fun Health Fact:

Pancakes are best eaten as soon as possible before they go rubbery, but if you're cooking for a crowd, keep them separate until you're ready to serve by layering them up between pieces of kitchen roll.[34]

Raw Mocha Brownies

Prep Time: 5 mins *Cook Time:* 30 mins

Equipment: Food processor, 20cm x 20cm (7.8" x 7.8") baking tin and parchment paper

Makes: 12

100g/1 cup x ground almonds
100g/1 cup x hazelnuts
12 x medjool dates, pitted
1tbsp x maple syrup
2tbsp x coconut oil
3tbsp x raw cacao powder
1 heaped tbsp x peanut or cashew
    butter
1-2tbsp x decaff espresso powder

Topping
1tsp x decaff espresso powder
    mixed with 1tsp x raw cacao
    powder

My friends love these healthy brownies when we get together. Make a tray and grab the biggest one!

1   Line the baking tin with parchment paper

2   Place the ground almonds and hazelnuts into a food processor and blitz together to form a fine powder

3   Add in the rest of the ingredients and pulse together until fully incorporated

4   Press the mixture into the prepared baking tin and smooth over the top with the back of a spoon

5   Set in the freezer for at least 30mins

6   When ready to serve, remove from the tin and lightly dust with the espresso and raw cacao powder mixture

Fun Health Fact

Hazelnuts are rich in anti-oxidants and are a source of folate, B-vitamin biotin, which promotes healthy skin and hair.[29]

Matcha Lime Cheesecake

Prep Time: 10 mins *Cook Time:* 15 mins *Setting Time:* 40 mins
Equipment: 18cm (7") springform tin and parchment paper

Serves: 8-10

This is your OMG-I-can-still-eat-cheesecake moment. This is a beautiful raw cheesecake which is totally gluten and dairy-free. It is my go-to for wowing people when they think 'I can't eat cakes'.

For the base:
175g/1¾ cups x ground almonds
1tsp x cashew butter
80ml/½ cup x coconut oil, melted
1tbsp x maple syrup

For the filling:
1tbsp x matcha powder
3 x limes, zest and juice
3tbsp x coconut cream
100ml/½ cup x coconut oil
4 x avocados
3tbsp x raw organic honey or
    maple syrup for vegans

Decoration suggestion
Edible flowers e.g. marigolds and
    pinks to decorate (see page
    143)

1. Line the base of the springform tin with parchment paper. In the bowl of a food processor add maple syrup, ground almonds and cashew butter then very briefly pulse together. While the food processor is running pour in the melted coconut oil until the dough comes together

2. Press the mixture into the base of the tin to form an even layer and place in the freezer for 20mins

3. While the base in setting in the freezer, begin to make the cheesecake filling. Add all the filling ingredients into a food processor and blend for 1-2mins until the mixture comes together and is smooth and creamy

4. Pour over the shortbread base, smooth over and set in the freezer for 20mins. Transfer to the fridge until ready to serve

5. When ready to serve, remove from the fridge and take out of the tin. Top with edible flowers and cut into slices

Fun Health Fact
Used for centuries by Buddhist monks to keep them focused during meditation, matcha is packed with antioxidants, calms the mind and is a great shot or flavour to anything from tea to ice cream![3]

Spiced Pink Bounty Bars

Prep Time: 15 mins Cook Time: 3 mins Setting Time: 40 mins

Equipment: 15cm x 15cm (6" x 6") tin lined with baking parchment, food processor

Makes: 12

Of course I would find a way to make a pink chocolate treat! I first learnt how to make bounty bars when I was working on a retreat in Tuscany. I have played around with them since, giving them a sweet spice and pink colour.

For The filling:
200g/2½ cups x desiccated coconut
10g/⅓oz x freeze dried raspberries
1tsp x Pitaya powder
1tsp x cinnamon
50ml/¼ cup x coconut oil
3tbsp x coconut cream
2tbsp x maple syrup

For The chocolate:
90g/1 cup x cacao butter chips
35g/¼ cup x raw cacao powder
2tbsp x maple syrup

To serve:
1tbsp x freeze dried raspberries, to sprinkle on top

1 Blitz the desiccated coconut in a food processor with the freeze dried raspberries and Pitaya powder until the mixture represents a coarse pink powder. Add the remaining ingredients and pulse until the mixture comes together

2 Press into the prepared baking tin to form an even layer and leave to firm in the freezer for 20mins

3 Remove from the freezer and cut into 12 even pieces

4 Heat the cacao butter chips, cacao powder and maple syrup over a gentle heat in a small saucepan and whisk together until it forms a smooth glossy chocolate

5 Spread the top of each bar with a generous layer of the chocolate, sprinkle over the freeze dried raspberries and place in the fridge to set for 20mins before serving

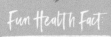

Fun Health Fact

Cinnamon contains large amounts of polyphenol antioxidants which can help protect the body from disease and have anti-inflammatory effects.[15]

Caramel Shortbread

Serves: 16-20

Who doesn't love a chocolate and caramel combo? This recipe is a crowd-pleaser and is such a treat with a cup of Magical Mylk (recipe found on page 25).

For the shortbread base:
225g/2¼ cups x ground almonds
1 heaped tsp x cashew butter
110ml/½ cup x coconut oil, melted
1tbsp x maple syrup or raw organic honey

For the caramel:
14 x medjool dates, pitted
2tbsp x coconut oil
1tbsp x maple syrup
150g/¾ cup x cashew butter
1tsp x ashwagandha powder (optional)
1tsp x flaky sea salt

For the chocolate:
100g/½ cup x cacao butter
2tbsp x raw cacao powder
3tbsp x maple syrup

1. For the base, add the ground almonds, cashew butter and maple syrup into a food processor and briefly pulse. Then slowly pour in the coconut oil while the motor is running and pulse until it all comes together

2. Press the mixture into the lined baking tin to form a flat layer and set in the freezer for 20mins

3. For the date caramel, blitz all the ingredients together in a food processor to form a thick caramel. Spread the caramel over the top of the shortbread base, using the back of a spoon that has been dipped in boiling water. Gently press down and smooth out the layer of caramel, ensuring it reaches all corners and is evenly spread across the shortbread base

4. Leave to set in the freezer for 20mins

5. For the chocolate, place all the ingredients into a small saucepan over a gentle heat and whisk together until it is smooth and glossy. Remove the caramel shortbread from the freezer and pour over the chocolate. Leave to set in the fridge for at least 20mins

6. Once set, remove from the fridge, take out of the baking tin and cut into pieces

Spiced Ginger Cookies

Prep Time: 10 mins *Cook Time:* 20 mins *Equipment:* Food processor, baking sheet lined with parchment paper

Makes: 10

200g/3 cups x gluten-free oats
50g/½ cup x ground almonds
1tbsp x ground ginger
1tbsp x ground cinnamon
1tsp x gluten-free baking powder
1tsp x salt
5tbsp x coconut oil
90g/¼ cup x maple syrup
2tbsp x almond milk

These are a **childhood favourite of mine**, adapted to make them skin friendly. I enjoy them best dipped into a cold glass of almond milk, sat by a warm fire.

1   Preheat the oven to 190C/375F

2   Place the oats into the food processor and blend into a powder, then mix them with the ground almonds, spices, baking powder and salt

3   In a jug whisk together the coconut oil, maple syrup and almond milk then pour this into the flour mixture, stirring well until it forms a stiff dough

4   Take a tablespoon of mixture and roll into a small ball, place on the lined baking sheet and flatten with the palm of your hand. Repeat until all the mixture has been used

5   Bake for 14-17mins until the cookies are firm to touch and golden

6   Leave on the tray until cool enough to eat

Fun Health Fact:

Ginger has long been used to treat digestive problems and circulatory disorders, and it also boosts our immune systems.[5]

Chicken (or Tofu) Pineapple & Veg Skewers

"A healthy outside starts from the inside."

— Robert Urich

Vegan Nachos

Prep Time: 30mins plus 1hr for soaking Cook Time: 15mins Equipment: Food processor

Serves: 4

Ah nachos. I studied abroad in California and everyone ate Mexican. My mouth would be watering to join in but I was afraid the tomatoes and dairy would trigger my skin. Then when I went to Canada my friend made me these amazing dairy-free nachos and I have never looked back. I have since made it my own – they are spicy, crunchy, creamy, super healthy and I'm so glad it's back on my menu.

For the cashew soured cream:
150g/5oz x cashews
2tbsp x raw cider vinegar
Squeeze of lemon

For the cheese dip:
1 x sweet potato, peeled and
    roughly chopped
2tbsp x coconut cream
2tbsp x nutritional yeast
1tbsp x tamari
Pinch of sea salt

For the guacamole:
2 x avocados, scooped
1 x lime, juiced
4 x spring onions, finely sliced
2tbsp x olive oil
Sea salt

For the salsa:
4 x tomatoes, deseeded and finely
    chopped
1 x red onion, finely diced
1 x red chilli, finely sliced
½ x lime, juiced
1 x small bunch fresh coriander,
    chopped
Sea salt

1 x quantity of black beans (recipe
    found on page 95)
200g/7oz x blue corn chips
Jalapeños to serve

1 For the cashew cream, place the cashews in a small bowl and pour over just enough boiling water to cover. Set aside for an hour to soften. Transfer the cashews along with their soaking water to a food processor and add the vinegar and lemon juice. Blend at high speed until smooth and creamy

2 For the cheese dip, bring a pan of water to the boil, add the sweet potato and cook for 5-7mins until tender. Drain and place in a food processor with the rest of the ingredients and blitz to a smooth cream

3 For the guacamole, place all the ingredients into a bowl, mash together with a fork and season to taste

4 For the salsa, mix together all the ingredients together in a bowl and season to taste. You can emit the tomatoes to make this recipe nightshade-free

5 For the black beans, turn to page 95 for the ingredients and method

6 To assemble the nachos, layer the corn chips on a platter then dollop over the beans, guacamole, salsa, cheese dip, soured cream and jalapeños

Cauliflower Pizza

Prep Time: 20 mins *Cook Time:* 1 hr *Equipment:* Food processor, baking sheet and parchment paper

Makes: 1 medium pizza

For The base:
1 x cauliflower (about 1kg), broken into florets
2tbsp x ground flaxseed
4tbsp x water
Salt

For The Topping:
8tbsp x pea pesto (recipe found on page 141)
4 x sun-dried tomatoes, chopped
1 x courgette/zucchini, peeled into ribbons
1 x red onion, finely sliced
1 x handful of black olives
100g/3½oz x vegan cheese (grated mozzarella style)
Handful of rocket/arugula to serve
Olive oil

Pizza was my high school food; I had a slice every lunchtime with friends and it has such happy memories. Then when I was 16 years old and started eliminating foods, this was one to go. But I really missed it and wanted to create a skin friendly version, so that's how this recipe was born. One of my all time favourites.

1   Preheat the oven to 180C/350F. To make the pizza base, place the cauliflower into a food processor and blitz until it has formed an even couscous like texture

2   Bring a large pan of water to the boil and blanch the cauliflower for a few seconds then strain using a fine sieve and rinse briefly under cold water

3   Place into a clean tea towel and squeeze out as much moisture as possible

4   Whisk the flaxseed with the water in a bowl then add the cauliflower and mix together to form a crumbly dough

5   Bring the dough into a ball with your hands and roll out between two pieces of baking parchment to create 1 medium pizza

6   Transfer these to a baking sheet and bake for 45mins until crispy and golden

7   Top the pizza with the pesto then scatter over the other ingredients, finishing with the cheese

8   Return to the oven for 8-10mins until the cheese has melted and the courgette/zucchini is starting to wilt

9   Scatter over the rocket/arugula and drizzle over a little oil to serve

Fun Health Fact

Cauliflower is full of antioxidants and phytonutrients that can protect against cancer. It also contains fibre to enhance digestion and choline, which is essential for learning and memory.[28]

Food For Sharing   135

Chicken (or Tofu), Pineapple & Veg Skewers

Prep Time 15 mins Cook Time 12 mins Equipment 12 bamboo skewers, baking tray

Serves: 4 / Makes 12

The perfect BBQ addition, healthy, fun and perfect for sharing. A simple party food that pleases everyone!

For the slaw:
1 x bunch spring onions, finely sliced
½ x white cabbage, finely sliced
2 x carrots, coarsely grated
2tbsp x sesame seeds
1tbsp x black sesame seeds
2tbsp x sunflower seeds
1tsp x chilli flakes
1 x lime, juiced
1 x small bunch fresh coriander, roughly chopped
3tbsp x toasted sesame oil
Sea salt

For the skewers:
3 x skinless chicken breasts or 450g/15oz x tofu, diced into 2½cm/1" chunks
½ x fresh pineapple (about 800g), peeled and sliced into 2½cm/1" chunks
2 x red onions, sliced into thin wedges
1tbsp x olive oil

1. Firstly, prepare the slaw. Place all the ingredients in a bowl and toss together well. Season with salt to taste

2. Thread the chicken/tofu, pineapple and onion onto 12 bamboo skewers. Brush them with a little sesame oil

3. Place the skewers on a baking tray under a hot grill/broiler for 10-12mins, turning regularly until they are beginning to char and the chicken/tofu is cooked through. Serve with the slaw

Fun Health Fact

The pineapple core is full of the healing enzyme bromeliad, a powerful anti-inflammatory used to treat bowel, digestion and joint problems.[16]

Lancashire Hotpot

Prep Time 25 mins *Cook Time* 1 hr *Equipment* Shallow casserole pan approx 30cm/12" diameter

Serves: 4

I'm a **Northern English girl** and **hotpot** was a classic family meal for us, so I had to include this warrior friendly version. It is great for winter and a perfect one-pot meal that everyone can help themselves to.

For The pickled cabbage
1 x red onion, finely chopped or
    sliced
1 x small red cabbage, finely
    shredded
100ml/3½fl oz x raw cider vinegar
2tbsp x raw honey
1tsp x caraway seeds
2tsp x sea salt

For The Hotpot
600g/1lb 5oz x grass-fed lamb
    neck, chopped into 2½cm/1"
    pieces or a mix of 200g/7oz
    x whole cooked chestnuts
    and 400g/14oz x button
    mushrooms
1 x onion, finely sliced
2 x leeks, roughly sliced
3 x carrots, roughly chopped
1 x bay leaf
1 x sprig of rosemary
2tbsp x chestnut flour
750ml/1½pt x chicken bone broth
    (recipe found on page 107) or
    good quality vegetable stock
4-5 x parsnips (depending on
    thickness), peeled and sliced
    very thinly into rounds
Salt
1tbsp x olive oil

1. Make the pickled cabbage a few hours before you want to eat. Place all the ingredients in a large pan and mix well

2. Bring to the boil, cover and simmer gently for 10mins then turn off the heat and leave to steep for 1hr. Strain away the excess liquid and store in the fridge

3. Preheat the oven to 170C/340F

4. In the casserole pan heat the olive oil over a high heat and fry the lamb for 3-5mins until brown all over. If using the chestnuts and mushrooms, fry over a medium heat for 5-7mins until they are browned

5. Turn down the heat and add the onion, leeks and carrots. Fry over a low heat for 5mins until golden and fragrant

6. Add the herbs, chestnut flour, a sprinkling of salt and stir well. Add the broth or stock, bring to the boil then remove from the heat

7. Layer the parsnips over the casserole in an even layer with as few gaps as possible

8. Cover with foil, transfer to the oven and bake for 40mins. Then uncover and cook for a further 10mins until the parsnips are golden

9. Warm the pickled cabbage through in a large pan and serve with the hotpot

Flowering Pasta

Prep Time: 13 mins Cook Time: 10 mins Equipment: Food processor

Serves: 4

For The pea pesto:
200g/7oz x peas
3 x garlic cloves, roughly chopped
60g/2oz x toasted pine nuts
100g/3½oz x rocket/arugula
1 x small bunch mint
1 x lemon, juiced
6tbsp x olive oil
Sea salt
Pepper

For The pasta:
200g/7oz x brown rice linguine
1tbsp x olive oil
Large handful of edible flowers
    e.g. borage, mint, chive,
    nasturtiums or whatever is
    available

Such a beautiful recipe to make and share with the ones you love. For a simple recipe adding edible flowers really does give it the wow factor. See page 143 to pick your preferred flowers.

1 To make the pesto, blanch the peas in boiling water for 2mins. Drain and refresh under cold water

2 Add the peas, garlic and pine nuts to a food processor and blend to form a rough paste. Add the rocket/arugula, mint, lemon juice and olive oil and blend again. Season with salt and pepper to taste

3 Bring a pan of water to the boil and cook the pasta for 8-10mins. Drain and toss with the olive oil

4 Stir through the pesto, place in a large serving bowl, scatter over flowers and serve

Fun Health Fact

Rocket/arugula leaves are tender and bite-sized with a tangy flavor. They contain more than 250 milligrams (mg) per 100 grams (g) of nitrate. High intake of dietary nitrate has been shown to lower blood pressure and reduce the amount of oxygen needed during exercise, enhancing performance.[1]

Top Tip:

Edible flowers can be frozen into your ice cubes. Use these in your drinks for the extra 'wow factor'.

Edible Flowers

I love **edible flowers** – they make any dish a beautiful masterpiece. I asked an expert gardener to help me write **this section**. Most of these are available at any good garden centre or online. Availability does vary from season **to season though**.

Tender (summer bedding needs frost protection)

Begonia Tuberosa – Can be used in salads to add colour. The petals taste pleasant. (contains oxalic acid)

Pelargoniums Odorata – One of the most useful plants for edible purposes. This is a must for any edible garden! Flowers can be added to salads, drinks and used for decorating cakes. The leaves are scented and can have a strong citrus, rose, pine and even cola aroma. The leaves are great for flavouring drinks!

Fuchsia – Hardy varieties are available but tend to produce smaller flowers. Both the flowers and berries are edible. The berries can be used in much the same way as other berries – they can be made into jams, compote or used as flavouring for ice cream.

Marigolds – Can be used to colour dishes in a similar way to turmeric and saffron. Just add petals or whole flowers to any dish to give some vibrant colour. Can also be used to colour rice. Mild flavour.

Calendula – Used in the same way as Marigolds.

Society Garlic – Use the flowers to flavour salads and rice, use the stems as a garlic substitute. The flower has a milder taste than the stems, which are quite strong.

Dahlia – A wonderful plant that grows with a wide range of different coloured flowers. The flowers can be added to dishes for decoration and as a bonus the tubers (bulb like root) can also be eaten.

Hibiscus – Some may survive outside in a sheltered, sunny location. The most common use is to strain the leaves to make Hibiscus tea.

Nasturtium – Bright yellow or orange, perfect for brightening up any dish. The flowers have a peppery taste.

Sunflowers – Use individual petals in salads. They have a slight nutty flavour.

Snapdragons – Add them to cakes or tables for decoration. They have a bitter taste so whilst edible, they aren't to everyone's liking.

Hardy (need no winter protection)

Lavender – Has a strong flavour. Can be used for flavouring cakes. Easy to dry and use as required all year round.

Roses – Another must in the garden! Little known, but roses are a very useful edible plant. The leaves can be made to make tea, the flowers are used for decoration and to garnish salads, and the flower buds can be eaten too before they open. However, wait longer and the hips are perhaps the best bit. Full of vitamin C and used to make jams or flavour things such as ice cream, simply slice the hip and remove the seeds just like a small pepper.

Primroses – Wide range of colours and the flowers are mainly used in salads and cake decoration.

Bellis Perennis – Daisy. Mainly used for cake decoration.

Monarda – Red or purple flowers that can be used to garnish salads. The leaves and flowers can be used to make tea.

Daylily 'hemerocallis' – Each flower only lasts for a day so don't feel bad picking them! Large flowers that are yellow or orange, they make beautiful decorations. The unopened flower buds can be stir-fried. Note: Don't confuse with lilies as they are not edible.

 **Heuchera** – Use the green, brown or purple leaves in salads.

 Carnations – Known as 'pinks'. The flowers come in a range of sizes, in red and pink colours. They are perfect for putting on top of cakes or adding to salads. They also look great in drinks.

 Salvia – Sage flowers make a useful addition to salads. Serve with meat dishes. The flowers can also be used to make tea.

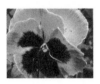 **Pansies and Violas** – An easy plant that provides masses of really pretty flowers. The smaller Viola flowers are more useful than the larger Pansy flowers. Add the flowers to salads or decorate cakes with them. Freeze them in ice cubes to add to drinks.

 Tulips – Use the individual petals in salads or for decoration.

 **Chrysanthemums** – Use the unopened flower buds to make tea and use the petals as a garnish.

 **Borage** – These blue flowers taste like cucumber. The flowers look great and are probably best used as decorations or for adding to drinks.

 **Clover** – Add the leaves to salads.

 Dandelion – Mainly thought of as a weed but very useful as an edible plant. Use the leaves in salads or to make tea. The flowers can be used in salads or as a decoration. They can also be fried with other herbs to make a snack or interesting starter dish.

You can also use the flowers of herbs. They tend to have a more delicate flavour than the leaves or stems.

"*I give myself permission to bloom unapologetically.*"

- Alex Elle

The HOPE Principles
– The Beauty of Eating Well™

You may recognise the key components of the HOPE Principles from The Beauty of Eczema™ book; Home, Optimism, Purpose, Pampering, Eating Well, Exercise and Ecotherapy.

The HOPE Principles provide a framework for living your best life beyond eczema. Each principle works like a piece of a jigsaw puzzle that nourishes your mind, body and soul. When I am living a balanced life following the principles, my skin GLOWS. So I have adapted these for this cookbook with a focus on how you can incorporate them into your life specifically when Eating Well.

H is for Home

Home is where your journey to eating well begins. Under Home comes 'environment', 'sleep' and 'declutter' but specifically in this cookbook, Home is all about creating a little sanctuary in your kitchen to create the best environment to begin nourishing yourself from within. There are certain essentials you'll need to make it easier for you to Eat Well and GLOW, so in order to help you declutter your mind (and kitchen), I have put together a list of pantry essentials, basic utensils and equipment to get you started.

Pantry & Cupboard Essentials

Flours:
Buckwheat flour
Rice flour
Chestnut flour
Teff flour
Almond flour

Noodles:
Buckwheat noodles
Brown rice noodles

Flakes/cereals:
Oat flakes
Quinoa flakes
Coconut flakes
Desiccated coconut
Buckwheat puffs
Rice puffs
Gluten-free tortilla chips

Crackers:
Rice crackers
Gluten-free oat crackers

Seeds:
Chia seeds
Flaxseed
Sunflower seeds
Pumpkin seeds

Nuts:
Cashew nuts
Almonds
Peanuts
Hazelnuts

Coloured superfoods:
Matcha
Chlorella
Blue spirulina
Pitaya
Cacao
Coconut water
Aloe vera gel
Vanilla/chocolate pea protein

Sweeteners:
Maple syrup
Honey
Vanilla stevia
Coconut sugar
Medjool dates

Tins/Jars:
Chickpeas
Lentils
Kidney beans
Cooked beetroot
Tahini
Full fat coconut milk
Nut butters
Sauerkraut
Kimchi
Sun-dried tomatoes
Canned tomatoes

Frozen foods:
Acai pulp
Mango
Blueberries
Strawberries
Banana
Gluten-free bread loaf
Frozen seafood
Frozen vegetables
Frozen fish

Condiments/Spices/Oils:
Turmeric
Ginger
Himalayan salt
Pepper
Mixed herbs
Mixed spice
Oregano
Thyme
Za'atar
Rosemary
Garlic
Tamari sauce (gluten-free soy sauce)
Cinnamon
Coconut oil
Olive oil
Sesame oil
Cider vinegar

Utensils and Equipment:
All the usual equipment from chef knives, to measuring spoons, chopping boards, pots, pans, measuring cups, baking sheet, tin, parchment paper and peelers

More specialised ones would be:

Nut milk bag
Blender
Spiralizer
Food processor
Juicer

Before cooking, set the scene and put those positive vibes into your food. Personally, I like to get vibes flowing by playing some of my favourite music and opening a window to let a fresh breeze in. If your family and friends can hear the uplifting music and feel the positivity coming from the kitchen, they may want to join in on all the fun and support you whilst cooking. Feel free to take inspiration and personalise this to suit your soul, it's all about creating a fun atmosphere for you and your loved ones to cook in.

1   Play your favourite, uplifting music

2   Invite Mother Nature indoors by letting some
    fresh air in or by growing flowers/herbs on your
    kitchen window sill

3   Keep an open door and encourage friends and
    family to cook with you

O is for Optimism

Gratitude journaling, visualisation and affirmations helped me develop an optimistic mindset when living a life beyond eczema. It was a game changer when I started thinking with a more positive mindset about both my eczema *and* my food. Re-framing my mind to think positively on what 'I CAN' eat rather than what 'I CAN'T' eat was so incredibly powerful. There is science to support that a positive mindset sends healing chemicals throughout the body. Approaching food in this way not only improved the condition of my skin, but it has helped me heal my relationship with food.

Warrior, I encourage you to start optimistically visualising the kind of cooking and food you want to enjoy. Focus on what you CAN have rather than what you can't. I get so excited when I find new dairy-free options and new wellness cafés popping up. Part of living optimistically is positively owning what is best for YOU. Take note in your

Positive Scribes Journal of the ingredients your body thrives on and enjoy every sensory stage of cooking, from the scent to the first mouthful.

I am a firm believer in **bio-individuality** – each of us has our own unique food and lifestyle needs. I thrive off colourful, mainly plant-based foods that are free from gluten, dairy and refined sugar. I also limit but don't totally eliminate nightshades and embrace anything that supports a healthy gut. This brings me JOY and explains why The Beauty of Eating Well™ focuses around these. I encourage you to take inspiration and listen to your inner wisdom and tailor these recipes to support your needs. Choose food that encourages a positive outlook towards your body and lifestyle.

P is for Purpose

Living purposefully and eating well is knowing that you deserve to nourish yourself with not only the foods you enjoy, but with what your body thrives on. Make it your purpose to own what is best for you and live by it. What you give to the world each day is so incredibly important, for not only you but those around you too. When living your purpose in life, allow yourself to mindfully sit down and enjoy a nourishing meal or take the time to share delicious food with your support network. You can fulfil your purpose so much better and serve the world on a greater level once you have given yourself the chance to refuel.

Top tips for eating more mindfully:

1   Put technology away and focus on your food

2   Eat slowly

3   Savour every single mouthful, noticing the flavours on your taste buds

P is also for Pampering

As well as preparing your food, cleaning up can also be made to be a comforting and soothing part of the cooking ritual. Keeping your hands safe and pampered throughout can make the simplest meal preparation feel the most luxurious. The products you use daily in your kitchen become a part of your daily skincare routine, so treat your skin and make life a little more comfortable for yourself.

To protect my sensitive skin when cooking, I like to use disposable biodegradable gloves and when doing the dishes I make sure to wear rubber gloves. I also like to pamper myself with my favourite natural hand wash and hand cream that I know work well for my skin. The more I can do to protect my hands whilst cooking makes the process of eating the prepared food much more enjoyable!

Look at pampering yourself as an essential rather than a treat because it's another magical puzzle piece of living a life beyond eczema. Give yourself a hand massage and give thanks for the delicious food you are about to eat.

"Eating well
is a form of
self respect."

E is for Eating Well, Exercise and Ecotherapy

Ecotherapy

From a young age, my happiest memories took place when I was hand in hand with Mother Nature. From running by the sea and growing fruit in the South of France, to climbing trees and playing in the Lake District with my siblings, I have always been a nature girl. I feel that when I'm in nature, I am connected to my true self. So, no matter where I am in the world, I always make time for self-care in the great outdoors because I have learnt how important it is for my glow.

Connecting with nature whilst eating a wholesome meal reminds me to cultivate an attitude of gratitude for the world we live in. Being able to partake in all of these wonderful foods that nature provides brings me so much joy. By simply taking your meal outside, sitting by the window or even bringing nature indoors with your favourite plant or fresh herbs, you're connecting yourself to Mother Nature.

Exercise

Exercise and eating well work together beautifully to sustain a positive mental and physical lifestyle. There are many ways to move your body to get those vibes and endorphins flowing, from high intensity training to a calming yoga flow. I personally enjoy both variations of exercise depending on how I feel each day. It's important to remember that small, gentle movements made throughout the day are equally as important as a heavy gym session.

Making small changes to your daily activity can have an amazing impact on your lifestyle and skin. Rather than driving to purchase ingredients for a healthy, nutritious meal, set yourself some time aside for self-care and make a conscious decision to walk instead. Not only will your daily step tracker thank you, but your mind, body and skin will too! The endorphins will make you feel magical and you'll feel incredible knowing you have exercised whilst focusing on the intention of eating well.

"If 'I' is replaced with 'WE', even illness becomes wellness."

Eating Well

The term 'eating well' to me means individuality, balance, joy, mindfulness and fun. Over the years I have discovered what food works best for me and what food doesn't. I have obsessed over food and I have now found a balance. I eat warmer, softer food in winter and cooler foods during the summer. I have taken a pinch from many diets and found my own way to eat. I encourage you to do the same. If there is one thing that has really stuck with me from my health coach and natural chef training, it is that we are all very different, unique individuals. We live in different places, climates, have different careers, support networks; so why would we all eat the same? I have been fortunate enough to live in different places throughout my life, had a variety of life experiences and I have found that my diet has adjusted with the locations, lifestyle and cultures. My advice to you is to tune into what works for you and adjust as needed. If you need guidance, the food diary in the Positive Scribes Journal is helpful. You can track what you eat each day and see how it makes you feel, then naturally you'll find your flow.

Another key part of 'eating well' for me is 'owning who I am'. I used to feel 'difficult' in certain situations, because my diet wasn't just like everyone else's. But I have now decided that part of living my best life beyond eczema is learning to 'fit out' rather than 'fit in'. I own my food choices with a smile and I encourage you to do the same. Feel proud every time you ask for the 'gluten-free' menu or if you ask for your food can be cooked without butter. Remember, the best person at taking care of you, is you. Your decisions deserve care and respect.

Stress Management and Support

Let's Make Eating Out Fun Again!

Managing to eat well from the comfort of your own home may seem easier to manage than eating out, but you deserve the confidence to go anywhere and feel prepared! Good news, I've learned from experience and put together my suggestions that will help you manage different eating out situations that you might find yourself in.

Us warriors have busy lives, right? You want to eat with your tribe, take a road trip, go on holiday and take work opportunities as and when. However, I know from experience that any big change in environment can suddenly pose food dilemmas. *I'm starving! But I don't want to eat something too random – what about my skin?* You can't help but think ahead – but you don't want to overthink, start fearing food again or make life awkward for hosts. Dilemmas! Like I said, the good news is that I've been here and done this angel and you can learn from my experience. Here are my suggestions:

Group Holiday

Ok, so I may have been the person that literally took their juicer on a holiday, but rest assured I have better ideas now! If you are renting a villa or staying in a holiday home, find out: do you have your own cooking facilities? If so, what are they? What type of food might be really fun and tasty to eat using them? Eating out local – what kind of cuisine do the locals enjoy? What dishes are they known for? What are the ingredients? Can you eat it, or can you make your own version with a slight tweak or variation? Do they have a food market nearby? What grows locally and in abundance? What wellness cafés can you explore? Get out your guidebook – or Google Translate – and find out how to say names, ingredients and how to pronounce them. Learn how to ask for things like 'dairy-free' and 'gluten-free'. A little work here goes a long way and you'll arrive for your holiday feeling refreshed and confident. It's also always good to have a back-up plan. So if you have room, pack a few staples in your suitcase – dairy/gluten-free protein bars, popcorn, oat/rice crackers, raw chocolate, small dairy-free milk, chia seeds, nuts and a gluten-free bread loaf (recipe found on page 67) are my kind of go tos.

Festivals/Concerts

I have lots of wellness, yoga, fitness and music festivals on my bucket list. I know all festivals are filled with fun but they also can come packed with sugary alcohol together with dairy and gluten laden foods.

Drinks – My approach to alcohol at festivals and concerts is usually to listen to my body. Sometimes I feel in a strong place with my skin and can enjoy one or two drinks (preferably gin and tonic, vodka soda or a glass of red wine) and I savour them, enjoy them, live in the moment, drink plenty of water in between and take a milk thistle supplement to support my liver ahead of the event. Other times I feel it is best to avoid alcohol altogether and that is when I step up on 'owning who I am' and decide to 'fit out'. I embrace fresh mineral water with a squeeze of lemon and focus on the enjoyment of the music. This is sometimes, and more often than not, best for my skin and I have learnt to be comfortable with my decisions. I hope this gives you the courage to listen to your body too.

Food – Invite everyone to your home for a tummy lining brunch (see the Lunch section on page 87 for ideas) or get the party started early with some healthy, tasty sharing platters (see page 131). Recently, my group of friends hit up a vegan café pre Spice Girls, which nourished our bodies and got us ready to dance the night away. Whatever makes you feel great, own it, and surround yourself with the friends that enjoy those things too, or at least support you!

Weddings/Occasion Meals Out

Thankfully over the years my friends have become really supportive of my mission of living a life beyond eczema and catering companies have made it easy for those with intolerances. Lately all I have to do is tick a box on the menu for 'dairy/gluten-free' and not have to worry. However, if that isn't the case for you and you find yourself at a big event, do what you can. Have a quick word with the waiting staff as they come round with the bread rolls – this is also a good time to enquire about the main course too. *"Can I have my main course cooked without butter please?"* These kinds of requests are no longer outrageous or unusual, plus you can often view menus online then call ahead with any questions – most people are very happy to cater for you. I once took my own drink of Kombucha to a wedding and everyone wanted to try it. You do you angel!

Cinema

Most cinemas are yet to catch up with the wellness scene, so my advice would be to bring your own treats and own it! I love cooking up the recipes from the snack and dessert section and munching them through the movie.

Petrol Station

Petrol stations used to be filled with only chocolate bars and crisps, but thankfully things have changed these days and they often do fresh fruit and protein bars which are made with all natural ingredients. I suggest getting what feels best for you.

Enjoying Food with Friends and Family

I've always been such a sociable person, happiest when surrounded by family or chilling with my friends; and I can't emphasise enough how lonely it made me not to join in and take part happily. Don't worry angel, I'm here to tell you it can all change overnight. When I realised **"eating a not so perfect meal in good company is more healing than a perfect meal eaten alone",** it changed my life forever and I hope it does for you too!

How To Approach It

Start from a positive frame of mind and think, 'I am so looking forward to seeing my friends or family and sharing a meal with them'. Think how lucky you are to have such a supportive group and be able to get together in this way. 'OK, it's my turn to cook, what can I make them that is really tasty, that we can all enjoy together?' Try cooking up something that's great to share (see page 131). Or, if you have been invited somewhere and someone else is wearing the chef's hat, then it's time to relax and own who you are. This is less about the food, it's about the joy of company. Focus on savouring the social side. Depending on how well you know the chef and how comfortable you are, speak up – ask for something without butter or for a gluten-free alternative. Fill up on vegetables, ask if you can bring anything to accompany the dishes and enjoy it! If you fancy a bit of what everyone else is having, which you wouldn't normally eat but it looks SO good, eat a mouthful (mindfully)! What feels right, usually is right. You know yourself, warrior. Listen to your body and mind, and go for it. Remember, you can get straight back to what works specifically for you. Remember, you can get straight back to what works specifically for you. But for now – be imperfectly perfect, living a balanced life and embracing all the nourishing vibes from the social interaction. I know it may seem daunting but it will become second nature and this is a HUGE part of living your best life beyond eczema.

"Happiness is the highest form of health."

— **Dalai Lama**

Glowing Skin Weekly Meal Plan

	Monday	Tuesday	Wednesday
Drinks	Hot Water with Fresh Lemon Green Glow Juice	Hot Water with Ginger & Honey Pink Glow Juice	Hot Water with Fresh Lemon Alkaline Me Up Juice
Breakfast	Avocado & Salmon on Toast	Chia Seed Pudding or Chocolate Monkey Smoothie Bowl	Grain and Nut-Free Chocolate Granola with Coconut Yoghurt
Lunch	Buckwheat Noodle Buddha Bowl	Crispy Haddock with Mint Potatoes	Baked Sweet Potatoes with Baked Beans & Slaw
Snack (optional)	Chocolate Bliss Balls	Banana & Oat Bars	Avocado on Oatcakes
Dinner	Chicken Bone Broth	Green Glowing Goddess Soup	Pad Thai
Dessert (optional)	Vanilla, Strawberry and Chocolate Nice Cream	Spiced Ginger Cookies with Almond Milk	Caramel Shortbread

"Actually, I can."

This meal plan has been created to get you started with incorporating 'eating well' into your lifestyle. These are all recipes from this book and those that I personally thrive on. I thought a little guide for the first week would give you some inspiration. Feel free to mix and match all the recipes. I can't wait to see what you make. Tag me on Instagram @thebeautyofeczema and @camilleknowles so I can see your beautiful creations and support you in living your best life beyond eczema.

Thursday	Friday	Saturday	Sunday
Hot Water with Fresh Lemon	Hot Water with Fresh Lemon	Hot Water with Fresh Lemon	Hot Water with Fresh Mint & Lavender
Vitamin A Booster Juice	Beautiful Blood Cleanser Juice	Maple Latte or Magical Warming Mylk	Red Glow Juice
Gluten-Free Porridge	Grain-Free Banana Bread or Grain-Free Bread	Pink & Green Quinoa Bowl or Tropical Bliss Smoothie Bowl	Blue Lagoon Magic Smoothie Bowl
Prawn Salad	Smoked Salmon Courgetti	Seabass with Cauliflower & Fennel	Flowering Pasta
Hummus & Veggie Sticks	Seeded Teff Crackers with Hummus Dip	Coconut Yoghurt with Berries	Grain-Free Bread
Comforting Cottage Pie or Thai Green Curry	Steak & Chips	Vegan Nachos	Cauliflower Pizza
Spiced Pink Bounty Bars	Raw Mocha Brownies	Matcha Lime Cheesecake	Banana Pancakes

UK to US Conversion Tables

Volume

U.S.	Metric	Imperial
¼ tsp	1.2 ml	
½ tsp	2½ ml	
1 tsp	5 ml	
½ tbsp (1¼ tsp)	7½ ml	
1 tbsp (3 tsp)	15 ml	
¼ cup (4 tbsp)	60 ml	2 fl oz
(5 tbsp)	75 ml	2½ fl oz
½ cup (8 tbsp)	125 ml	4 fl oz
(10 tbsp)	150 ml	5 fl oz
¾ cup (12 tbsp)	175 ml	6 fl oz
1 cup (16 tbsp)	250 ml	8 fl oz
1¼ cup	300 ml	10 fl oz (½ pint)
1½ cup	350 ml	12 fl oz
2 cups (1 pint)	500 ml	16 fl oz
2½ cups	625 ml	20 fl oz (1 pint)
1 quart	1 litre	32 fl oz

Weight

U.S.	Metric
¼ oz	7 g
½ oz	15 g
¾ oz	20 g
1 oz	30 g
8 oz (½ lb)	225 g
12 oz (¾ lb)	350 g
16 oz (1 lb)	450 g
2 lb	900 g
4 lb	1 kg

Oven

Fahrenheit (°F)	Celsius (°C)	Gas Number	Oven Terms
225	110	¼	Very Cool
250	130	½	Very Slow
275	140	1	Very Slow
300	150	2	Slow
325	165	3	Slow
350	180	4	Moderate
375	190	5	Moderate
400	200	6	Moderately Hot
425	220	7	Hot
450	230	8	Hot
475	250	9	Hot
500	260	10	Extremely Hot
550	290	10	Broiling

Length

U.S.	Metric
3.9 inch	10 cm
4.7 inch	12 cm
5.9 inch	15 cm
7.0 inch	18 cm
7.8 inch	20 cm
8.6 inch	22 cm
9.8 inch	25 cm
11.0 inch	28 cm
11.8 inch	30 cm

Glossary of Terms

Blue Spirulina: This brightly coloured, freshwater algae contains a powerhouse of nutrients which flush out toxins and boost your entire immune system. It is also known for building endurance levels and energy.

Cacao Nibs: Cacao nibs are made from chopping up cocoa beans that have been fermented and dried but not roasted.

Cacao Powder: Raw cacao powder is made by cold-pressing unroasted cocoa beans, which retains the living enzymes and removes the fat (cacao butter). Cacao is the purest form of chocolate you can consume and is high in antioxidants.

Caraway Seeds: Caraway seeds are highly aromatic and have a distinctive mild anise flavour that adds a subtle licorice hint to many dishes. If you've ever eaten rye bread, you have no doubt tasted caraway seeds.

Chia Seeds: Chia seeds are the edible seeds of Salvia hispanica, a flowering plant in the mint family. Their protein and glucose are key for the body's repair system.

Chlorella: Chlorella is a type of algae and one of the most nutritionally dense foods in the world. It is naturally high in vitamin B12 and vitamin D and brilliant at helping to rid the body of toxins and improve cholesterol and blood sugar levels.

Dairy-free: A dairy-free diet means avoiding anything that is not nut or plant based, and is made from the milk of animals such as goat, sheep or cow.

Flaxseed: One of the oldest crops in the world, brown or golden flaxseed (or linseeds) are good sources of many nutrients. Their health benefits are mainly due to their content of omega-3 fats, lignans and fibre.

Gluten-free: Gluten is a protein found in wheat, barley and rye and is present in any food or drink made from or containing these grains. This includes pasta, bread, crackers, seasoning, spice mixes and couscous. People with coeliac disease or dermatitis herpetiformis could benefit from following a gluten-free diet throughout their lives.

Goji Berries: The bright red berries, sometimes called 'wolfberries', have a woody, slightly raisiny taste – a bit like cranberry. They are packed with vitamin C and antioxidants and are brilliant for healthy skin and the immune system.

Hemp Oil: Hemp oil is obtained by pressing hemp seeds. Cold pressed, unrefined hemp oil is dark to light green in colour, with a nutty flavour. Compared with other culinary oils, hempseed oil is low in saturated fat and rich in polyunsaturated fat.

Matcha: For centuries Buddhist monks used this green tea powder, rich in natural antioxidants, to focus during meditation. Now this versatile superfood, one of Japan's best-kept secrets, is growing increasingly popular, and popping up in everything from bread and brownies to lattes.

Nigella Seeds: One of the oldest spices in the world, nigella seeds are not generally included in cooking but once you are familiar with the taste, the black dots add interest as a finishing touch to plain rice and to vegetables, especially such sweet ones as carrots and parsnips. They can also be used in salad dressings.

Nightshade-free: Nightshade vegetables form part of the Solanaceae plant family and include potatoes, peppers, tomatoes and aubergines (or eggplants). A nightshade-free diet will eliminate all of these plus multiple herbs and spices, including cayenne pepper, chilli powder, paprika and crushed red pepper, plus condiments such as ketchup, hot sauce and salsa.

Nut-free: Nut allergies can be fatal so it's vital that anyone on a nut-free diet carefully reads any food labels. The most common nut allergy is to peanuts but sufferers should also avoid almonds, Brazil nuts, cashews, chestnuts, hazelnuts, macadamia nuts, pecans, pistachios and walnuts.

Paleo: People following a paleo diet will only eat foods that would have been available in the Paleolithic era, between 2½ million and 10,000 years ago when modern agriculture developed. Nowadays followers will only eat what could have been hunted or gathered back then, including fish, seafood, lean meats, fruit, vegetables, nuts and seeds. They avoid dairy, legumes, grains, soft drinks containing sugar and processed foods are off limits.

Pitaya: Otherwise known as dragonfruit, the tropical superfood Pitaya can be either sweet or sour, depending on the species. The most common form, which is smaller than a cantaloupe, red, and covered with spiky growths, can protect the body from aging and diabetes. It is also a great immunity and digestion booster.

Probiotic Capsules: Probiotics are live bacteria and yeasts promoted as having various health benefits. They're usually added to yogurt or taken as food supplements, and are often described as "good" or "friendly" bacteria.

Probiotics are thought to help restore the natural balance of bacteria in your gut (including your stomach and intestines) when it's been disrupted by an illness or treatment.

Tahini: Tahini (or tahina) is a condiment made from toasted ground hulled sesame. It is served by itself or as a major ingredient in hummus, baba ghanoush, and halva. Tahini is used in the cuisines of the Eastern Mediterranean, the South Caucasus, and the Middle East, as well as parts of North Africa.

Tamari: Tamari soy sauce is traditionally made with little or no wheat, whereas wheat is one of the 4 common ingredients in regular soy sauce. It has the same bittersweet tangy flavour and is a great accompaniment to noodle based dishes and fish.

Teff: Teff is a tiny seed from Ethiopia that packs a big punch. "The new quinoa" is packed full of fibre, is great for our muscular, nervous and cardiovascular systems, plus it contains 69% of our daily value of magnesium and 10% of our daily value of vitamin B6 (Pyridoxin) in one serving.

Vegan: A vegan diet is a plant-based diet avoiding all animal foods, such as meat, shellfish, dairy, eggs and honey.

Zaatar: A spice mix born in the Middle East, this flavoursome combination consists of thyme, sesame seeds, sumac and salt. Variations sometimes include marjoram or oregano, rather than thyme. These herbs and spices contain a wealth of powerful nutrients and organic compounds, including thymol, gallic acid, carvacrol and quercetin. They combine to improve mood, memory and aid indigestion and chronic diseases.

References

1. Neal's Yard Remedies Healing Foods: Eat Your Way To A Healthier Life by Susannah Steel
2. Superfoods: The Food and Medicine of the Future by David Wolfe
3. The Book of Matcha: The Superhero of Tea by Louise Cheadle and Nick Kilby
4. The Chickpea Cookbook by Heather Thomas
5. The Ginger Book; Ultimate Home Remedy by Stephen Fulder
6. https://www.huffingtonpost.ca/2014/02/06/teff-benefits-_n_4740219.html
7. https://www.medicalnewstoday.com/articles/283476.php
8. https://draxe.com/nutrition/article/maple-syrup-nutrition/
9. https://draxe.com/nutrition/vegetables/red-cabbage/
10. https://draxe.com/nutrition/vegetables/watercress/
11. https://www.bbcgoodfood.com/glossary/basil
12. https://www.medicalnewstoday.com/articles/283018.php
13. https://www.bbcgoodfood.com/howto/guide/health-benefits-apples
14. https://www.bbcgoodfood.com/howto/guide/health-benefits-almonds
15. https://www.bbcgoodfood.com/howto/guide/health-benefits-cinnamon
16. https://www.bbcgoodfood.com/howto/guide/health-benefits-pineapple
17. https://www.bbcgoodfood.com/howto/guide/health-benefits-spirulina
18. https://www.bbcgoodfood.com/howto/guide/health-benefits-sweet-potato
19. https://www.bbcgoodfood.com/howto/guide/health-benefits-watermelon
20. https://www.bbcgoodfood.com/howto/guide/ingredient-focus-coconut-milk
21. https://www.healthline.com/nutrition/benefits-of-acai-berries
22. https://www.healthline.com/nutrition/green-peas-are-healthy
23. https://www.louisehay.com/18-amazing-health-benefits-bone-broth/
24. https://www.medicalnewstoday.com/articles/263405.php
25. https://www.medicalnewstoday.com/articles/277627.php
26. https://www.medicalnewstoday.com/articles/282769.php
27. https://www.medicalnewstoday.com/articles/284823.php
28. https://www.medicalnewstoday.com/articles/282844.php
29. https://www.medicalnewstoday.com/articles/323807.php
30. https://www.olivemagazine.com/guides/nut-benefits-expert-guide-to-nuts/
31. https://www.telegraph.co.uk/food-and-drink/features/what-are-the-health-benefits-of-eating-red-meat/
32. https://www.theguardian.com/lifeandstyle/2013/jan/24/dates-truly-fruit-of-paradise
33. https://www.theguardian.com/lifeandstyle/2013/sep/07/why-broccoli-health-benefits
34. https://www.theguardian.com/lifeandstyle/wordofmouth/2011/mar/03/how-to-cook-perfect-pancakes
35. https://www.womenshealthmag.com/food/a19992452/health-benefits-of-ginger/

Acknowledgements

Thank you to you, a beautiful warrior who has decided to read this book, and learn new ways to live a life beyond eczema. You deserve to eat with joy and experience glowing skin.

Thank you to my family, friends and other half, for helping me find joy in food again and for encouraging me to share my wisdom with the world. You are loved and appreciated beyond belief.

Thank you to my dream team, I am so grateful for you! For all the hours you've poured into helping me bring this book to life. We've moved mountains to create this and I know you are just as proud of it as I am.

Lots of love and positive vibes,

Camille x x

Index

- thebeautyofeczema.com/Instagram
- thebeautyofeczema.com/Facebook
- thebeautyofeczema.com/YouTube
- thebeautyofeczema.com/Pinterest

#thebeautyofeatingwell
www.thebeautyofeczema.com

lots of love and positive vibes xx

Food Photography: Clare Winfield
Lifestyle Photography: Clare Winfield
Lifestyle Photography: Catherine Booty
Food & Prop Stylist: Polly Webb-Wilson
Assistant Food Stylist: Hattie Arnold
Makeup & Hair Stylist: Stephanie Swain
Gardening Expert: David Fearnley
Creative Direction: Summer Whittaker
Design & Art Direction: Sam Pearce
Project Management: Carol Carson

Also by Camille Knowles:

The Beauty of Eczema™ Book
Positive Scribes Journal
Positive Scribes Self-Care Affirmation Cards

Lightning Source UK Ltd.
Milton Keynes UK
UKHW050632150720
366335UK00009B/118